AF240876

Treatise on
the three impostors
Moses, Jesus, Mohammed

The spirit of Spinoza

TREATISE ON
THE THREE IMPOSTORS
Moses, Jesus, Mohammed

Max Milo

Max Milo Editions
Collection Essais-Documents, Paris, 2023
www.maxmilo.com
ISBN : 978-2-31501-098-1

Editor's Introduction

This work is some four centuries old. It is not only topical, and burning, but it constitutes a renewed object of astonishment. This is, moreover, the reason why we are publishing it.

When she heard of the *Treatise on the Three Impostors*, reports the English bibliophile Richard Smith, the former Queen Christine of Sweden, the same one who had once hired René Descartes as a professor of philosophy, offered a small fortune to obtain a copy; in vain. The work existed then only in manuscript form; she would probably have been satisfied with it; she did not get it. It was not published for the first time until 1712 in Rotterdam, in that land of intellectual freedom which was the Netherlands. Christine had then been dead for twenty-three years - the point is interesting, as we shall see below. There are only four copies left of the seventy of the original edition, due to Charles Levier.

Until the French Revolution, this impertinent text excited the sagacity of the scholars. Undoubtedly, Christine's brokers were not fast: one counts no less than twenty-six handwritten copies in France and two abroad, before the printing. And one could compose a whole volume of the comments that this firebrand aroused. Who was the philosopher who so strongly denounced the three great religions of the Book and called their proponents, Moses, Jesus and Mohammed, impostors? The question as much as the text deserved at the time and deserves today at least as much interest as some considerations topped with the philosophical appellation. But when it was finally published in 1999 in France, none of the augurs of the national press thought it appropriate to talk about it. In these times of fatwas, it is better to remain covered. Especially since here, the imprudent person who would have reported on it would have incurred a triple fatwa that would have triggered the ire and violent disaffection of his readers. One will forgive us the indignation, undoubtedly polemical, which is ours, but finally, it seems legitimate to us.

Among their virtues, these texts - the plural is quite intentional - demonstrate, indeed, that intellectual freedom was much more ardent in the seventeenth and eighteenth centuries than it seems to be in the twentieth and twentieth. Alas, the debates on the *Treatise of the Three Impostors do* not go beyond a small circle of academics who, for the sake of their fortune and peace of mind, do not care about fashions and literary prizes. Nevertheless, we submit today, once again, this text to the public. For the convenience of the reader, we have modernized the spelling as much as possible without altering the text, and replaced certain words and phrases, incomprehensible to the modern reader, by their equivalents. These alterations are indicated by square brackets.

The *Treatise on the Three Impostors* first appeared in 1712 under the title *L'Esprit de M. Benoît de Spinosa*, preceded by a biography entitled *La Vie de M. Benoît de Spinosa*. These two works, of very dissimilar contents, were paired only for their common reference to Spinoza. Whose are they? The question has lost none of its relevance in three centuries. As far as the first one is concerned, let us rule out Spinoza's own participation for chronological reasons: indeed, *La Vie de M. Benoît de Spinosa* refers to events after the philosopher's death, in 1677: the presence of the Prince of Condé in Utrecht, «at the beginning of the last wars», and this was in 1678.

According to the preface of the first modern publication, Richard H. Popkin, in Italian, by Giulio Einaudi in 1994, the author of *La Vie de M. Benoît de Spinosa* was Jean-Maximilien Lucas (1636 (?) - 1697), a gas merchant whose family had come from Rouen and had been exiled to Holland.

The second book, which follows, poses problems that are less easy to solve, and even involves a mystery. In his *Dictionnaire historique* published in The Hague in 1758, Prosper Marchand concluded that the author of *L'Esprit de M. Benoît de Spinosa was* a certain Jan Vroesen. Marchand was a scholar, editor, bibliographer, bookseller, and writer, and one of the most knowledgeable figures on the movements of ideas and authors in Northern Europe. It was certainly not lightly that he put forward the name of Vroesen so firmly.

A few biographical details have come down to us from his biography: born on October 4, 1672 in Rotterdam, son of a notable of the city, Adriaen Vroesen, Jan Vroesen became chargé d'affaires in France in 1701 and 1702, at the age of 29; then he was appointed counselor of the court of Brabant in The Hague, a position he held until his death in August 1725. Not much more is known about him, and nothing about his physical appearance.

If we were to stick to this information, however, we might be embarrassed. Indeed, if he is indeed the complete and only author of *L'Esprit de M. Benoît de Spinosa*, Vroesen would have been of a fulminating precocity: Christine of Sweden died in exile in Rome in April 1689 and had no money left to acquire expensive manuscripts. Moreover, if Smith is to be believed and if she knew of the existence of the famous manuscript, it must have been around 1687. Vroesen was then only 15 or 16 years old. At that tender age, he would have embraced not only Spinoza's work, but also the entire European philosophical landscape in order to produce these pages, whose strength and modernity remain astonishing.

15 years old, is it possible? It is hard to believe that a very young man was capable of the audacity of the text that follows, and of its violence in the rejection of the three religions. Rejection of Revelation, rejection of the Incarnation, rejection of Inspiration, the message is virulent. According to this text, in fact, all religions are alike, a thesis which already contradicts the originality of Christianity; but above all, these religions, including paganism, are decoys at the service of political power. Of course, it was in the Holland of the Free Thought, but the

enterprise was not without danger, even in these privileged places: on July 19, 1674, a decree of the Dutch Court of Justice had condemned together two major works, whose reputation lasts far beyond legal and theological anathemas, Spinoza's *Tractatus theologico-philosophicus* and Hobbes' *Leviathan*, though less openly subversive. There was reason for a teenager to be cautious.

In fact, if Vroesen dipped into the writing of this book, it was neither at 15 nor at 16 years of age, but much later, perhaps after his stay in Paris, undoubtedly inflamed by the thinkers he had met there. Still based on Marchand's information, one would then conclude that Vroesen made in the *Treatise of the Three Impostors* a synthesis of the antireligious tendencies of the time.

It is here however that the mystery appears. There was already at least one *Treatise on the Three Impostors*, a version of which, according to Silvia Berti, to whom we owe a remarkable presentation of the two works, was the work of a lawyer from Reims, Marc-Antoine Oudinet. And Marchand speaks, indeed, of a text «which one saw running the world in manuscript since approximately forty or fifty years». And there was even another clandestine text of the same spirit and almost of the same title, *De Tribus Impostoribus*. Would Vroesen have taken up a theme, if not a manuscript that was agitating the intellectual circles of the time? That would be almost accusing him of plagiarism without any foundation.

But if one understands the anecdote about Christine of Sweden - she was still on the throne when she heard about the famous manuscript, and it was not Vroesen's - one wonders why Marchand attributed to the latter the work published by Levier in Rotterdam in 1712.

It is even less understandable that the publishers of *L'Esprit de M. Benoît de Spinosa first* changed the title of the work in the 1721 republication in Frankfurt am Main, «at the expense of the translator» (which is not to be found today, by the way), and compressed the original eight chapters into six, thus eliminating any reference to Spinoza, and then later added extracts from thinkers who were no doubt in the same vein, Pierre Charron and Gabriel Naudé, but who had nothing to do with the text attributed to Vroesen. It is true that in those days people were less fussy about the rights of authors, but this is still a lot of levity.

More serious and more enigmatic: the 1712 edition is adorned with a presumed portrait of Spinoza on the frontispiece, which bears no resemblance to the other proven documents that represent the philosopher: it did not fool the contemporaries, who recognized a variant of a portrait of René d'Anjou, king of Naples.

Until the French Revolution, literate Europe was full of memoirs, hypotheses and questions about the true author of the *Treatise of the Three Impostors*. One even came to suspect Frederick II of Prussia, a notorious anticlerical, of being this author. This was to forget that the Great Frederick was born in the same year that the Rotterdam edition was published.

The bibliographic and philosophical enigma cannot make us forget that this is a tribute to the great philosopher. His spirit floats, indeed, through these vigorous pages. Some authors nowadays even tend to believe that the author of *Ethics* is at the origin of this mysterious book. Certainly, several passages reflect a careful reading of Spinoza, such as the sixth chapter *On Spirits Called Demons*, which comes straight out of the *Short Treatise* on the Theory of the Igneous Soul, or the first two chapters on the popular conception of God, which are borrowed from him. Specialists will delight in detailing other borrowings. But the virulent disdain for the Old and New Testaments, for example, which is evident in many passages of the *Treatise,* does not correspond at all to Spinoza's ideas or tone, nor does the irreverent atheism.

Could it be that Levier, the first editor of the Treatise, and the mysterious Vroesen extracted from the Spinozian archives in Holland, «probably from the Rieuwertz fund», notes the critical edition of the Bibliothèque de la Pléïade, a selection of texts that they transformed as they pleased? This is, in the end, the hypothesis that seems most plausible. For despite the mysteries and manipulations, if not the forgeries, the shadow of Spinoza floats across the enterprise and the text obviously comes from Holland. The hypothesis is reinforced by the publisher's striking desire to pay homage to Spinoza by publishing in the same volume *The Life* and *Mind of M. Benoît de Spinosa*. This is undoubtedly an exaggerated homage to the philosopher, awkwardly reinforced by the borrowings from Pierre Charron and Gabriel Naudé. It evokes those Rubens of which we know from the studio books that the great painter only added a few touches here and there, but which he signed nevertheless.

It emerges that the *Treatise of the Three Impostors* appears as a collective anthology of the resistance to religion in the Europe of the Enlightenment. Spinoza is only the emblem, but he is nevertheless omnipresent.

These are therefore pages of particular importance in the history of Western thought that we present here, in the hope that a wide audience will finally have access to them. At a time when the wars of religion no longer speak their name, but no less victims.

Max Milo

THE SPIRIT OF MR. BENEDICT OF SPINOZA

> If for lack of a faithful brush,
> Of the famous Spinoza one did not paint the features,
> Wisdom being immortal,
> His Writings will never die.

Warning

There is perhaps nothing which gives strong minds a more plausible pretext for insulting religion than the manner in which its defenders act. On the one hand they treat their objections with the utmost contempt, and on the other they solicit with the most ardent zeal the suppression of the books which contain these objections which they find so contemptible.

It must be admitted that this procedure is detrimental to the cause they are defending. Indeed, if they were assured of her goodness, would they fear that she would succumb by supporting her only with good reasons? And if they were full of that firm confidence which the truth inspires in those who believe they are fighting for it, would they have recourse to false advantages and wrong ways to make it triumph? Would they not rest solely on its strength, and, sure of victory, would they not willingly expose themselves to the battle of equal arms against error? Would they not like to leave everyone free to compare the reasons on both sides, and to judge by this comparison on which side the advantage lies? If this liberty is taken away, will it not give the unbelievers reason to imagine that their arguments are feared, and that it is easier to suppress them than to show their falsity?

But although we are persuaded that the publication of their strongest statements against the truth, far from harming it, would only serve to make its triumph more brilliant, and their defeat more shameful, we did not dare to go against the tide by publishing *The Spirit of Mr. Benedict of Spinoza.*

So few copies were printed that the work will hardly be less rare than if it had remained in manuscript.

It is to the clever people, capable of refuting it, that we will take care to distribute this small number of copies. There is no doubt that they will beat the author of this monstrous writing, and that they will overthrow from top to bottom the impious system of Spinoza on which the sophisms of his disciple are founded. This is the aim of printing this treatise, from which the libertines will draw their captious arguments.

It is given without any cuts or softenings, so that these gentlemen will not say that the difficulties have been made more difficult in order to make the refutation easier. Besides, the gross insults, the lies, the calumnies, the blasphemies, which one will read there with horror and execration, refute themselves, and can only turn to the confusion of the one who advanced them with as much extravagance as impiety.

PREFACE OF THE COPYIST

Baruch or Benedict of Spinoza, has acquired such a disreputable name in the world in relation to his doctrine, and to the singularity of his sentiments in matters of religion, that one must hide when one wants to write about him, or in his favor, with as much care, and use as many precautions, as if one had a crime to commit. However we will not make a mystery of admitting, that we copied this writing according to the original, whose first part treats of the life of this character[1], and the second provides an idea of his spirit.

The author is unknown, in truth, although the one who composed it was one of his disciples, as he explains himself clearly enough. However if it were allowed on conjectures to lay some foundation, one could say, and perhaps with certainty, that all the work is of the fact of the late Mr. Lucas, so famous by his quintessences, and even more by his manners and his way of life.

Be that as it may, the work is rare enough to deserve to be examined by people of good mind; and it is with this sole purpose in mind that we have taken the trouble to make a copy. This is the goal we have set ourselves, leaving others the care of making some reflections on it, which they will judge appropriate.

---

1. In the present edition, the first part entitled *La Vie de M. Benoît de Spinosa* is not reproduced.

Chapter I
About God

I. Although it is important for all men to know the truth, very few nevertheless know it, because most believe themselves incapable of seeking it on their own, or do not want to take the trouble. Thus we should not be surprised if the world is full of vain and ridiculous opinions, nothing being more capable of giving them course than ignorance. Indeed, it is ignorance that is the sole source of the false ideas that we have of the divinity, of the soul, of spirits, and of all the errors that depend on them. It is a custom that has prevailed, to be satisfied with the prejudices of birth, and to refer to persons paid to support the opinions received, and consequently interested in persuading the people, whether they are true or false.

II. What renders the evil without remedy is that, after having established the insipid ideas that one has of God, one teaches the people to believe them, without examining them, and that one gives them aversion to the true scholars, who could make known to them the errors in which they are immersed. The supporters of this nonsense have succeeded so well in this respect that it is dangerous to fight them. It is too important to them that the people be ignorant to suffer that they be disabused of their ignorance. Thus one is forced to disguise the truth, or to sacrifice oneself to the rage of false scholars and interested souls.

III. If the people could understand the abyss into which ignorance throws them, they would soon shake off the yoke of those venal souls who, for their own interests, keep them there. For this he would only have to use his reason; it is impossible that by letting it act, he would not discover the truth. It is true that to prevent him from using it, it is represented to him as a guide who leads astray those who abandon themselves to its conduct, and as a will-o'-the-wisp, whose deceptive light leads to the precipice. But these people, whose profession is to declaim against reason, do not leave, after having shouted against it, and after having maintained that it is entirely perverted, to make all their efforts to put it on their side, and to persuade that those who fight their feelings are not reasonable. Thus, falling into perpetual contradictions, it is difficult to know what they claim. What is certain is that right reason is the only light that man should follow, and that the people are not as incapable of using it as they are persuaded to be. If as much effort were made to rectify their false reasonings and to disabuse them of their old prejudices as is done to maintain them in some and confirm them in others, they would gradually open their eyes, become susceptible to the truth, and learn that God is nothing like what they imagine.

IV. Indeed, there is no need for high speculations, nor for penetrating very far into the secrets of nature; all that is needed is a little common sense to see that God is neither angry nor jealous; that justice and mercy are false titles attributed to him; and that nothing that the prophets and apostles have said about him constitutes either his nature or his essence. Speaking plainly, and telling it like it is, it is certain that these people were neither more skilful nor better instructed than the rest of mankind in these matters. Far from that, what they say about it is so crude that one must be a people to believe it. The thing is obvious in itself; but to make it even more sensitive, let us see if there is any appearance that they were made differently than other men.

V. As to their birth and the ordinary functions of life, it is agreed that they had nothing above the human; that they were born of men and women; and that they sustained their lives in the same way as we do. But as for their minds, it is claimed that God directed them by immediate inspiration, and that their understanding was far more enlightened than ours. It must be admitted that the people have a great tendency to be blinded. They have been told that God loved the prophets better than the rest of mankind; that He communicated Himself to them in a special way, and they are as firmly persuaded of this as if it were demonstrated to them. And without considering that all men are alike; that they all have the same principle to which all beings are equal, he believes that these people were of an extraordinary temperament, and made on purpose to speak the oracles of God. But besides the fact that they had neither more spirit than the common man, nor a more perfect understanding than the rest of men, what do we see in their writings, which obliges us to have this feeling about them? Most of what they said is so obscure that we cannot hear it, and in such a bad order that we can see that they did not understand themselves and that they were very ignorant. What gave rise to the belief that we have of them, is that they boasted of having immediately from God all that they announced to the people. An absurd and ridiculous claim, since they themselves admit that God spoke to them only in dreams. For dreams being natural, and moreover, a state of slumber, a man must be very vain, or very foolish, to boast that God spoke to him at that time, and that he who adds faith to it must be equally credulous, to believe, against all appearance, that dreams are oracles. Even supposing that God made himself heard to someone by dreams, visions, or by other means, no one, nevertheless, would be obliged to believe him, because one would always have reason to fear that this man had been deceived by some impostor, or that he had deluded himself, or finally that he had the intention of deceiving others. So we see that in the old Law, the prophets were not held in such high esteem as they are today. When they were tired of their chatter, which most often tended only to divert the people from the obedience they owed to their legitimate kings, they were silenced by various tortures. Jesus Christ succumbed in this way, because he did not have, like Moses[2], an army at his heels to defend his opinions.

Add to this the fact that the prophets were so accustomed to contradicting one another, that sometimes, in four hundred, not one of them was true[3]. Moreover, it is certain that the purpose of their prophecies, as well as of the laws of the most famous legislators, was to eternalize their memory, by making the people believe that they were conferring privately with God. The most astute politicians have always used it in this way, although this ruse did not succeed for those who, in imitation of Moses, had no means of providing for their safety.

VI. Having said this, let us examine the ideas that the inspired ones and the prophets have had of God, and we shall see how crude and contradictory they are. According to them, God resembles man, whom they say he made in his own image. Like him, he has eyes, ears, nostrils, a mouth, arms, hands, feet, a heart and entrails. He is susceptible of the same passions, of love, jealousy, hatred, joy, sadness, pleasure, pain, hope, fear, aversion, anger, fury, revenge.

Here is the contradiction. They say that God is a pure spirit who resembles nothing corporeal. Yet Micah[4] sees him seated, Daniel[5] dressed in white and in the form of an old man, and Ezekiel[6] as fire.

There is not even his Spirit that has not been seen in a corporeal figure. John the Baptist[7] sees him in the form of a dove, and the apostles[8] in the form of tongues of fire. Moreover, they give him human members, and say that he made man in his own image and likeness[9],

---

2. Moses suddenly killed twenty-four thousand men for opposing his Law. (Num 25, vol. II to IX.)

3. In the first Book of Kings (1 Kings 22:6), Ahab, king of Israel, consulted four hundred prophets, all of whom were mistaken in their prophecies.

4. 1 R 22, 19.

5. 1 R 7, 9.

6. 1 R 1, 27.

7. Mt 11:16.

8. Acts 2, 3.

9. Gen 1:26.

as we have just noted. They teach that he is invisible[10], that no man ever saw him[11], nor can he see him and live[12], however Jacob[13], Job[14], Moses[15], Aaron, Nadab, Abihu, the seventy elders of Israel, Manoah[16] and his wife, most of the prophets and an infinite number of other men have seen him in their lifetime, the others will see him in the next world[17], we will see him there face to face[18], we will be like him[19], and we will see him as he is.

On the one hand, they tell us that God is good, gentle, charitable, tender, pitiful, benign, merciful, patient, that he does not take pleasure in the death of the wicked[20], but rather in his conversion. On the other hand, that he is severe, terrible, dreadful, a consuming fire, that he takes pleasure in the destruction of the wicked[21], that he laughs and mocks at their calamity, and that he does not answer them when they cry out to him[22]. In Genesis[23], man is represented as the master of doing good and not sinning, while St. Paul[24], on the contrary, teaches that he has no power over concupiscence without a very special grace. It is said in Exodus[25] that God will punish the iniquity of the fathers on the children until the fourth generation, and in Ezekiel[26] that he will not make the son bear the iniquity of the father.

---

10. Heb 11:27; 1 Tim 1:17.
11. Jn 1:18.
12. Ex 33, 20.
13. Gen 32:30.
14. Gen 42:5.
15. Ex 21:9-11.
16. Jdg 23, 22.
17. Mt 5:8.
18. 1 Cor 13, 12.
19. 1 Jn 3, 2.
20. Ez 18:23-30.
21. Dt 28, 63.
22. Pr 1:26-28.
23. Pr 4, 7.
24. Rm 7, 18; 9 10.16.
25. Rm 20, 5.
26. Rm 18, 20.

Samuel[27] says, after the Book of Numbers[28], that God does not repent, Jeremiah[29] and Joel[30], on the contrary, say, the one, that he repents of the good and evil he had said he would do to a nation, or to a kingdom, the other, that he repents of having afflicted.

Moreover he repented for having made the man[31], for having set up Saul as king[32], and for the evil he had said he would do to the Ninevites[33].

These are the feelings that these people with dreams, inspirations, ecstasies, visions, revelations, have of God. This is what they want us to believe. But to believe such contradictions, one would have to be as crude and as stupid as those who, in spite of Moses' tricks, believed that a calf was the God who brought them out of Egypt.

Without dwelling on the reveries of a people brought up in servitude, and among superstitions, let us finish this chapter, and conclude from what we have said, that ignorance has produced credulity, the credulity of lies, from which all the errors that reign today have emerged.

<hr>

27. 1 Book 25, 29.
28. 1 Book 23, 19.
29. 1 Book 18, 7-10.
30. 1 Book 2, 13.
31. Gen 6:6-7.
32. 1 S 15, 2.
33. Jon 3, 1 o.

Chapter II
Reasons Which Have Led Men to Imagine an Invisible Being, or What Is Commonly Called God

I. Those who are ignorant of physical causes have a natural fear, which proceeds from the doubt in which they are, whether there is a power capable of harming them, or of helping them. Hence the inclination they have to pretend to invisible beings, that is to say their own ghosts, whom they invoke in adversity, whom they praise in prosperity, and of whom they finally make themselves gods.

As the visions of men go to infinity, they have created an innumerable number of deities, and have imagined that they were favorable or not, according to whether they did good or bad.

For example, when nature afflicted them with storms, barrenness, plagues and other such accidents, they believed that these evils were only happening to them because they had angered these deities by their offenses.

This chimerical fear of invisible powers is the seed of religions, which each one forms according to his own fashion. The politicians, to whom it was important that the people be imbued with similar fears, have made the belief in the vengeful gods of the violated divine and human laws, a fundamental law of their states, and by the apprehension of a terrible future, they have led their subjects to obey them blindly.

II. The source of the gods being found, men believed that they were like them, and that, like them, they made all things for some end. For they unanimously say that God made nothing but for man, and conversely, that man is made only for God.

This prejudice being general, let us see why men have so much inclination to embrace it, to show then that it is from there that they have taken occasion to form an idea of good and evil, of merit and sin, of praise and shame, of order and confusion, of beauty and ugliness

III. It is not the place here to deduce these ideas from the nature of the human mind; it will suffice for our purpose that we lay down as our foundation a principle that cannot be denied by anyone. This principle is that all men are born in profound ignorance concerning the causes of things, and that all they know is that they have a natural inclination to seek what is useful and convenient to them, and to avoid what is harmful.

From which it follows, first, that men feel in themselves that they can will and wish, and falsely imagine that this is sufficient to make them free. This is an error they fall into all the more easily, since they do not bother to find out what causes them to will and to wish, because they are incapable of thinking about it, nor of thinking about it, even in their dreams.

Secondly, it follows that men, doing nothing but for an end which they prefer to anything else, have as their aim only to know the final causes of their actions; that having known them, they are satisfied, seek nothing more, and imagine that there is no longer any reason to doubt.

Finding then in them, and outside of them, a quantity of means to achieve what they wish, having, for example, eyes to see, ears to hear, a tongue to speak, teeth to grind, hands to touch, feet to walk, fruits, vegetables, animals to nourish them, a sun to enlighten them, they formed this reasoning: that there is nothing in nature which is not made for them, and of which they cannot dispose.

Moreover, considering that they did not make the world, they thought they were justified in imagining a supreme being who made it for them as it is. For after having convinced themselves that this world could not have been made by itself, they concluded that it was the work of one or more gods, who destined it for the pleasure and use of man alone.

On the other hand, the nature of the gods being unknown to them, men judged of themselves that they were susceptible to the same passions and weaknesses as themselves, and on this basis, they imagined that they had made the world only for men, and that they were extremely dear to them. And as all inclinations are different, each one has endeavored to worship God according to his mood, to draw his blessings upon himself, and to make all nature serve his appetites.

IV. By this means, this prejudice having become superstition, it has taken root to such an extent, that the crudest people have believed themselves capable of penetrating into the final causes, as if they had a perfect knowledge of them; so that instead of showing that nature does nothing in vain, they have on the contrary shown that God and nature were dreaming as well as men.

So that we may not be accused of exaggerating things, let us see, I pray you, how far they have pushed their false reasoning on this matter. Having experienced that, in the midst of many comforts which nature made them enjoy, an infinite number of inconveniences, such as storms, earthquakes, illnesses, hunger, thirst, came to disturb the sweetness of their life, instead of concluding that nature had not been made for them alone, they attributed all these evils to the wrath of the gods, whom they represented as being irritated against them because of their sins. And although daily experience taught them otherwise, and an infinite number of examples proved to them that goods and evils were common to the good and the bad, nevertheless they could not get rid of such an ancient and inveterate prejudice. The reason for this is that it was easier for them to remain in their natural ignorance than

to give up the old system of final causes and invent a new and more
plausible one.

V. This prejudice led them to another, which is to believe that the
judgments of God were incomprehensible to them, and that it is for
this reason that the knowledge of the truth is above the human mind.
This error would still exist if mathematics and other sciences had not
destroyed this prejudice.

VI. We shall not need long speeches to show that nature proposes
no end, and that all final causes are only human fictions. For this
purpose, we need only show in two words that this doctrine takes away
from God the perfections attributed to him. Here is how we prove it:

If God acts for an end, either for himself or for another, he desires
what he does not have, and it must be admitted that there was a time
when God, not having what he acted for, wished to have it, which is to
make a God destitute.

And in order not to omit anything that might support this argu-
ment, let us oppose it with the reasoning of those who hold the opposite opinion, and we shall see that it is founded solely on ignorance. If,
for example, a stone falls on someone and kills him, they say that the
stone must have fallen with the intention of killing the man, since this
can only have happened because God willed it. If you reply that it was
the wind that caused the stone to fall at the same time as the man was
passing by, they ask you why the man was passing by at the same time as
the stone was falling? If you reply that the wind was strong at that time,
because the sea had been rough for the previous few days, even though
there was no agitation in the air, and that this man had been asked to
go and eat at a friend's house, and was going to the appointment, they
ask you again, because they never go, why this man was invited to his
friend's house at that time rather than at another time? Thus making
an infinite number of questions, to try to make them confess that the
only will of God, which is the asylum of the ignorant, is the cause of
this fall. In the same way, when they see the structure of the human

body, they fall into admiration, and conclude, as they are ignorant of the causes of such a marvel, that it is a supernatural work, in which the causes known to us can have no part.

Hence anyone who wants to know the causes of miracles in depth, and to penetrate the natural causes as a true scholar without amusing himself by admiring them in ignorance, is considered a godless person and a heretic, through the malice of those whom the common people recognize as interpreters of nature and of God. These mercenary spirits know only too well that the ignorance which holds the people in astonishment is what keeps them going, and what preserves their credit.

VII. Men, having thus assumed the ridiculous opinion that everything they see is made for them, have made it a point of religion to relate all things in the world to their interest, and to judge their value by the profit they derive from them. Hence they have formed these notions, which serve to explain the nature of things, namely good, evil, order, confusion, hot, cold, beauty, ugliness, which in the end are not what they imagine. As on the other hand they claim to have their free will, they believed themselves entitled to decide of praise and shame, of sin and merit; calling well all that turns to their profit, and what concerns the divine worship and the evil, or on the contrary, what is convenient neither to the one, nor to the other.

Those who are ignorant of the nature of things and who have no other idea of them than the one they form by the help of the imagination, which they take to be the understanding, imagine an order in the world, which they believe to be such as they imagine it to be. For men are made in such a way that they believe things to be well or badly ordered, according to whether they find it easy or difficult to imagine them when the senses represent them.

Indeed, since we are more attracted to what is least tiring to the imagination, we are easily persuaded that we are justified in preferring order to confusion, as if order were something other than a pure effect of the imagination of men. So that to say that God made everything in order is to attribute to him, as to man, the faculty of imagination. If it

CHAPTER II REASONS WHICH HAVE LED MEN TO IMAGINE AN INVISIBLE BEING is not, perhaps, in favor of the human imagination, that God created the world in the way that is easiest to imagine, even though there are a hundred things that are far beyond the powers of the imagination, and an infinite number of others that throw it into disorder, because of its weakness.

VIII. With regard to the other notions, they are pure effects of the same imagination, which have no reality, and which are only the different modes of which this power is capable. For example, if the movement which objects impart to the nerves by means of the eyes is pleasant to the senses, we say that these objects are beautiful. That smells are good or bad, flavors sweet or bitter, that which is touched hard or soft, sounds harsh or harmonious, depending on whether the smells, the flavors strike and penetrate the senses pleasantly or unpleasantly. Until then, some have believed that God is capable of enjoying melody, and that the heavenly movements are a harmonious concert. This is a clear proof that everyone believes things to be as he imagines them, or rather that the world is purely imaginary.

That is why it is no wonder that there are hardly two men of the same opinion, and that there are even some who take pride in doubting everything. For although men have one body, which is similar in many things, it differs in many others, so that what seems good to one man seems bad to another, and what pleases this one displeases that one. From this it is easy to infer that feelings differ only with respect to fantasy; that understanding has little part in them, and that finally the things of the world are a pure effect of the imagination alone. But if, instead of relying on imagination, one consulted the lights of the understanding and mathematics, and did not go further than what one can conceive by the help of natural lights, everyone would agree on the truth, and judgments would be more uniform, and more reasonable than they are.

IX. It is evident, then, that all the reasons which the vulgar are wont to use when they attempt to explain nature, are only ways of imagining, which prove nothing less than what they claim. And as these reasons are given names as real as if they existed elsewhere than in imagination, I call them, not beings of reason, but pure imaginations; seeing nothing easier than to answer the arguments which are founded on these notions, and which are objected to as follows.

If it were true that the universe was a flow and a necessary continuation of the divine nature, from where would come the imperfections and defects that we notice in it? For example, corruption, which fills everything with a bad smell, so many unpleasant objects, so many disorders, so many evils, so many sins, and so many other similar things? It is nothing, I say, easier than to refute these objections.

For we must not assign more perfection to things than is appropriate to their nature and essence, and they are not more or less perfect, simply because they please or displease the senses, or are useful or useless to human nature. Moreover, we can only judge the perfection of any being as long as we know its essence and nature. But in order to shut the mouth of those who ask why God did not create all men without exception in such a way that they could be guided by the lights of reason alone, it is sufficient to say that he did not lack the material to give each being the degree of perfection that was most suitable for it, or, to speak more properly, because the laws of nature were so ample and so extensive that they could be used to produce all the things of which an infinite understanding is capable.

CHAPTER III
WHAT GOD IS

I. Up to now we have fought against popular prejudices about the divinity; but we have not yet said what God is. If we are asked, we will answer that He is an absolutely infinite being, one of whose attributes is to be an eternal and infinite substance. The extension or quantity being finite, or divisible, only when we imagine it to be so. For matter being everywhere the same, the understanding does not distinguish parts. For example, water, as water, is imagined to be divisible, and its parts separate from one another; although as a corporeal substance, it is neither separable nor divisible. Finally, water, as water, is subject to generation and corruption, although as a substance it is subject neither to the one nor to the other. Thus matter and quantity have nothing that is unworthy of God. For if everything is in God, and if everything necessarily flows from his essence, it is absolutely necessary that he be such as what he contains; since it is contradictory for all material beings to be contained in a being that is not material. And so that one does not believe that this opinion is new, Tertullian, one of the first men that the Christians had, pronounced against Appelle that what is not body is nothing. And against Praxeas, that all substance is a body, without this doctrine having been condemned in the first four ecumenical and general councils[34].

II. These sentiments are simple, and even the only ones that a good and healthy understanding can form of God. However, there are few who are satisfied with such simplicity. The coarse people are accustomed to the flatteries of the senses, and demand a God who resembles the kings of the earth. This pomp and splendor, which surrounds them, dazzles them in such a way that to take away all hope of going after death to swell the number of heavenly courtiers, to enjoy the same pleasures that one has enjoyed here below at the court of kings, is to take away their consolation and the only thing that prevents them from despairing in the miseries of life.

One wants a just and avenging God, who punishes and rewards in the manner of kings, and consequently a God susceptible to all human passions and weaknesses. We give him feet, hands, eyes and ears, we do not want a God constituted in this way to have matter. They say that man is his masterpiece and even his image, but they do not want the copy to be like the original. Finally, the God of today's people is subject to many more forms than the Jupiter of the pagans.

The strangest thing is that the more this nonsense contradicts and shocks common sense, the more the common people revere it. They stubbornly believe what the prophets have said, even though these visionaries were to the Hebrews what augurs and diviners were to the pagans, and what astrologers and fanatics are to us.

The Bible is consulted as if God explained himself in a particular way, although it is full of impertinent and ridiculous fables. Witness

---

34. These first four councils are: 1- That of Nicaea, held in the year 325 under the emperor Constantine the Great, and under Pope Silvester; 2- The first of Constantinople, held in the year 381 under the emperors Gratian, Valentinian and Theodosius, and under Pope Damasus; 3- The first of Ephesus, held in the year 431 under the emperors Theodosius the Younger and Valentinian, and under Pope Celestine; 4- That of Chalcedon, held in the year 451 under the emperors Valentinian and Marcian, and under Pope Leo I.

what is told of a serpent[35] and an ass[36] that spoke; of a woman changed into a statue of salt[37]; of a king metamorphosed into a brute beast[38]; of a Nazarene[39] who tears a lion to pieces, who kills a thousand men with the jawbone of an ass, who tears off the posts and bars of the gates of a city and carries them on his shoulders, who breaks the strongest ropes with which he is bound, who overturns a great building by embracing the pillars on which he is supported, all by a marvelous strength that resides in his hair; of a prophet[40] to whom the ravens brought food twice a day, who lived on one meal for forty days and forty nights of walking, who divided the waters of a river by striking them with his cloak, and passed through the middle on dry ground, who, finally, was taken up to heaven by a whirlwind in a chariot of fire, harnessed to horses of fire ; and of another prophet[41] who sojourned three days and three nights in the belly of a fish, where he breathed so comfortably that he sang a hymn.

In spite of all these childish tales, and an infinite number of others of which this book is full, people persist in canonizing it, and they do not want to pay attention to the fact that it is only composed of a fabric of fragments sewn together at different times, and given to the public at the whim of the rabbis[42], who only produced them after having approved some and rejected others, according to whether they found them conforming or repugnant to the Law of Moses.

Yes, such is the folly and stupidity of Christians, that they would rather spend their lives idolizing a book which they took from an

---

35. Gen 3:1-5.
36. Num 22:29-30.
37. Gen 19:26.
38. Dan 4:32-36.
39. Jg 14-16.
40. 1 R, 17-19, 2 Liv. II.
41. Jon 2.
42. The Talmud says that the rabbis deliberated whether to remove the Book of the Prophets and the Book of Ecclesiastes from the number of books in the Bible. They left it out because they found some places where it speaks highly of the Law of Moses. They would have done the same with the prophecies of Ezekiel, which would have had to be cut out of the Sacred Catalogue, if a certain canon had not had the skill to reconcile them with the same Law.

ignorant people, a book in which there is neither order nor method, which no one hears, so confused and ill-conceived is it, Such is, I say, their folly, that they would rather worship this phantom than listen to the natural law which God, that is to say nature, as the principle of movement, has written in the hearts of men.

All the other laws are only human fictions and pure illusions forged, not by demons or evil spirits, but by the skill of princes and ecclesiastics, those, to give more weight to their authority, those, to enrich themselves by the flow of an infinity of chimeras which they sell dearly to the ignorant.

As far as the laws of the Christians are concerned, they are founded only on a book whose original is nowhere to be found, and whose copies differ essentially in a thousand places from one another. Finally, on a book which contains only supernatural things, that is to say, impossible things, and whose rewards and punishments which are proposed for good and bad deeds only concern a future life, lest fraud be discovered in this one. No one has ever returned from the other to tell us about it.

Thus the people, always floating between hope and fear, are held to their duty by the opinion that God has made men only to make them eternally happy or unhappy. It is this opinion that hope and fear have given rise to an infinite number of religions, of which we shall speak[43].

---

43. The Bible.

CHAPTER IV
WHAT THIS WORD RELIGION MEANS
HOW AND WHY SO MANY OF THEM HAVE
CREPT INTO THE WORLD

I. Before the word *religion* was introduced into the world, people were obliged to follow natural laws, that is, to conform to right reason. This instinct alone was the bond to which men were attached. This bond, simple as it was, united them so that divisions were rare. But since fear had made them suspect that there were gods, and invisible powers, they raised altars to these imaginary beings. And renouncing the lights of nature and reason, which are the sources of true life, they bound themselves by vain ceremonies and superstitious worship to the phantoms of their imagination. It is from these sacred bonds, formed by fear, that comes this word Religion, which makes so much noise in the world. Men having thus admitted invisible powers which had all power over them, they worshipped them to bend them and imagined moreover that nature was a being subordinated to these powers. Hence, they imagined it as a great mass, or as a slave, which only acted according to the order that these powers gave it. Since this false idea had struck their minds, they had nothing but contempt for nature and reserved all their respect for these so-called beings, whom they named their gods. From this came the ignorance in which so many peoples are plunged, and from which the true scholars, however deep it may be, could withdraw them if their zeal were not crossed by those who lead these blind people and who live only on impostures. But although there is little appearance of success in this enterprise, one must not for that reason abandon the side of truth. Even if it is only in consideration of those who have secured themselves from the symptoms of such a great evil, a generous soul must tell it like it is.

II. The fear that made the gods also made religion; and since men got it into their heads that there were invisible angels, who were the causes of their good or bad fortune, they gave up common sense and reason, and took their chimeras for so many divinities that took care of their conduct. After having forged gods for themselves, they wanted to know of what nature they were, and finally imagined that they must be of the same substance as the soul.

Then, having persuaded themselves that it resembled the ghosts that appear in mirrors or during sleep, they believed that their gods were real substances, but so thin and so subtle that to distinguish them from bodies, they called them *spirits*, although bodies and spirits are indeed one and the same thing. They do not differ from each other, for a spirit and incorporeal being is an incomprehensible thing. The reason is that every spirit has a figure of its own, and that it is understood in some place, that is to say, that it has limits, and consequently that it is a body, thin, loose and subtle as it may be.

III. The ignorant, that is to say most men, having fixed the substance of their gods in this way, tried to penetrate by what means these invisible beings produce their effects. But not being able to do so, because of their ignorance, they believed their conjectures, judging blindly the future by the past, although they saw neither connection nor dependence.

In all that they undertook, they considered the past and foretold the future for good or for bad, according to whether the same undertaking had formerly succeeded or not. Thus Phormion having defeated the Lacedemonians with the battle of Naupacte, the Athenians raised another captain of the same name after his death. Hannibal having succumbed under the arms of Scipio, nicknamed the African, the Romans, because of this good success, sent in the same province another Scipio against Caesar, which succeeded neither to the Athenians, nor to the Romans. Thus, after two or three experiments, several nations attached to places, objects and names their good or bad fortune. Others made use of certain mysterious words, which they called enchantments, and believed them to be of such efficacy that they could, by their virtue, make trees speak, make a man out of a piece of bread, and metamorphose everything that appeared before them.

IV. The invisible powers being established in this way, at first men revered them only as they do their sovereigns, that is, by marks of submission and respect, such as are presents, prayers and the like. I say, at first; for nature does not teach to use in this meeting bloody sacrifices, which were instituted only for the sustenance of the priests and ministers destined to the service of these beautiful gods.

V. This seed of religions, namely hope and fear, by dint of passing through the passions, judgments and various councils of men, has produced that great number of bizarre beliefs which are the cause of so many evils, of so many barbarous cruelties, and of so many revolutions which occur in the States. The honor and the great revenues that were attached to the priesthood, as they have since been attached to the ministry and to ecclesiastical offices, flattered the ambition and the avarice of cunning people, who took advantage of the stupidity of the people and gave so well in their weakness, that they insensibly made themselves a sweet habit of incensing the lie and hating the truth

VI. The lie having been established, and the ambitious ones primed by the sweetness of being above their fellow men, they tried to make a name for themselves, by pretending to be friends of these invisible gods

that the common people feared. In order to succeed, each one forged
them in his own fashion and took such a license to multiply them that
one found one at every step.

VII. The formless matter of the world was called the god Chaos.
The same honor was given to the sky, the earth, the sea, the fire, the
winds and the planets. It was done to men and women; but the calf,
the dog, the swine, the crocodile, the serpent, the onion, the birds, the
reptiles, in a word all kinds of animals and plants had the best part.
Each river, each fountain bore the name of a god, each house had its
own, each man had his genius.

Finally, everything was full of spirits, shadows and demons, both
above and below the ground. It was not enough to pretend to have
deities in every conceivable place, one would have thought to offend
the time, the day, the night, the concord, the love, the peace, the victory,
the restraint, the rust, the honor, the virtue, the fever, the health One
would have thought, I say, to make insult to these beautiful deities,
if one had not raised temples and altars to them. Then, one began to
revere one's own genius, which some invoked under the name of muse.
Some, under the name of fortune, adored their own ignorance. The
others baptized their debaucheries of the name of cupid, their anger of
the name of fury, in a word, there was nothing which did not carry the
name of a god, or of a demon.

VIII. The founders of the religions, having been aware that the basis
of their impostures was the ignorance of the people, forgot nothing to
maintain it. The worship of images, in which they pretended that the
gods lived, seemed to them very appropriate for this, and they gave all
their care to establish it on durable foundations. For this purpose they
set up altars to these gods who deigned to manifest themselves to men
in their simulacra, they built them superb temples, instituted sacrifices,
feasts, ceremonies in their honor, established priests, ministers to serve
them, assigned ministers to serve them, and so on, ministers to serve
them, assigned to these ministers, in addition to the tithes, the best

pieces of the sacrificed animals, the best share of the fruits, vegetables, grains offered on their altars, and thereby engaged these low and venal souls to make use of a cult which was so useful to them. And these sacrifices, of which the gods had only the smoke, these tithes, these offerings were then considered as holy things, destined for the use of the sacred mysteries, so that no one would have the audacity to claim them, nor the temerity to touch them.

To better lure the people, these priests claimed to be prophets and made people believe that they were able to penetrate the future through the trade they boasted of having with the gods.

As nothing is more natural to man than the desire to know his destiny, these impostors were too clever not to take advantage of this inclination and to omit a circumstance so advantageous to their purpose. Some settled in Delos, others in Delphi, and elsewhere; where, by ambiguous oracles, they answered the requests, which one made to them. The women even got involved. Indeed, the Romans had recourse in the great calamities to the Books of the Sybils.

Fools and madmen were considered enthusiasts, and those who pretended to have dealings with the dead were called necromancers. Others read the future through the flight of birds or through the entrails of animals. Finally, the eyes, the hands, the face, an extraordinary object, everything seemed to them to be a good or bad omen. It is so true that ignorance receives such an impression as one wants, when one has the secret to take advantage of it.

Chapter V
About Moses

I. The ambitious, who have always been great masters in the art of deceit, have all followed the same path in establishing their laws. In order to force the people to submit themselves to them, they have persuaded them, with the help of the ignorance which is natural to them, that they had received them either from a god or from a goddess.

This is how the legislators have used it. They have all made their laws descend from some divinity and have tried to make people believe that they themselves were more than men. This is what one will be convinced of if one takes the trouble to read without prejudice what we are going to say about the four most famous of them, namely, Moses, Numa Pompilius, Jesus Christ and Mohammed.

II. The famous Moses, grandson of a great magician, according to the report of Justin Martyr, having made himself chief of the Hebrews, who were expelled from Egypt by edict, because they were infecting the whole country with the rancidness and leprosy with which they were spoiled, was one of those who made the most skilful use of this stratagem. After six days of marching in a painful retreat, he ordered these miserable banished people to consecrate the seventh day to God, by a public rest, in order to make them believe that God favored him, that he approved of his domination, and that no one would have the

audacity to dispute it with him. There were never people more ignorant than those, and consequently more credulous. In such a beautiful
opportunity to show off his rare talents, he made them believe that
God had appeared to him, that it was by his order that he was taking
their direction, that he had chosen him to govern them, that they
would be his special, privileged people, to the exclusion of all other
nations, provided that they believed and did what he told them. And to
convince them of his divine mission, he performed some subtle tricks in
their presence, which they took for miracles. Thus these poor wretches,
dazzled by his illusions and delighted to see themselves adopted by the
master of the gods at the end of a hard servitude, applauded Moses, and
swore to obey him.

III. His authority being confirmed, he thought of perpetuating
it; and under the pretext of establishing a supreme cult to serve God,
whose lieutenant he claimed to be, he made Aaron his brother and his
children the heads of the royal palace, that is, of the place where the
oracles were given out of the sight and presence of the people. Then he
did what was always done in new establishments, that is, wonders and
miracles, which dazzled the simple and stunned some, but caused pity
to those who were penetrating and read through his impostures. From
time to time he withdrew to a solitude, under the pretext of going there
privately to confer with God; and by this pretended immediate contact
with the divinity, he attracted unbounded respect and obedience.
However, however clever this legislator was, he would have had
difficulty in making himself obeyed, if he had not had force in hand.
Deceit, without weapons, rarely succeeded. Indeed, among so many
subjects whom he had had the art of enslaving, there were some who
were enlightened enough to see through his tricks, and brave enough to
reproach him that under the false appearances of justice and equality,
he had seized everything; that the sovereign authority being attached
to his blood, no one had the right to claim it; that finally, he was less
their father than their tyrant On these occasions, Moses, as a skilful
politician, destroyed these strong spirits without quarter and spared

none of those who criticized his government. With these precautions and by coloring his tortures with the name of divine vengeance, he lived always absolute.

And to finish as he had begun, that is to say, as a deceiver and impostor, he dug himself an abyss in that solitude where he was withdrawing alone and rushed into it, so that when his body was not found, it would be believed that God had taken it away.

He was not unaware, however, that the memory of the patriarchs who had preceded him was held in great veneration, even though their tombs had been found. But this was not enough to satisfy an ambition like his, he had to be revered as a god, on whom death had no hold. Indeed, this was the purpose of what he had said at the beginning of his reign: that he was established by God, the God of Pharaoh.

After him, Romulus[44], Elijah[45], Empedocles[46] and those who, like them, had the foolish vanity to eternalize their name, also hid the time of their death, so that one believed them immortal.

---

44. Romulus drowned himself in the goat marshes, so that, not finding his body, it was believed that he had been taken to heaven and deified.

45. See Chapter 2. A 2. Books of Kings.

46. Empedocles, famous philosopher, rushed into the sighs and volcanoes of Mount Etna to make believe, like Romulus, his rapture in heaven.

CHAPTER VI
OF NUMA-POMPILIUS

I. Numa-Pompilius, man learned in the Laws, was chosen, all Sabine that he was, to succeed Romulus. Although the Roman people had elected him unanimously and his election had been confirmed by all the senators, he still wanted the gods to be consulted on this choice and only accepted the kingship after they had made it known by celestial omens that they approved of him. He worked during a reign of more than forty years to soften the fierce morals of the Romans, by turning their minds to religion. He considered that the surest way to reign absolutely over ignorant, coarse and superstitious men, such as were the first inhabitants of Rome, was to inspire in them the greatest fear of the gods that it was possible. To succeed, he judged that the fiction of some miracle would be necessary; and as he had to deal with a people who already admitted as articles of divine faith the answers of the oracles and the predictions of the augurs and haruspices, he had no difficulty in imposing it to him.

He easily persuaded that the nymph Egeria had dictated to him the Laws and the institutions which he gave to him; and by this fraud, he knew to attach it to its duty by bonds all the more strong and all the more respectable that they were estimated sacred and divine.

II. But although in these coarse times, the credulity of the Romans was great, it was however still nothing compared to that of these same Romans of the polite centuries. Indeed, the latter had appropriated the gods, the beliefs and the superstitions of all the nations, which they had overcome. They had in particular adopted the theology of the Greeks, who believed, that Minerva was born of the head of Jupiter, and Bacchus of his thigh. That Eristonius and Myrrha were generated from this father of the gods, without mothers, and that on the contrary, Vulcan and Mars were sons of Juno, without fathers. Quinachus, Aeacus, Hercules, Alexander and an infinity of others were sons of Jupiter, and that Perseus was born of this god and the virgin Danae. The fecundity of a virgin was not incredible for people who admitted as divinely revealed truths an infinity of more absurd and contradictory things. Moreover, they perhaps held this last opinion from the Egyptians, who believed that the spirit of God, *pneuma qeon*, could engross a woman.

Chapter VII
About Jesus Christ

I. Jesus Christ, who was not ignorant of the maxims and knowledge of the Egyptians, took up this opinion and believed it to be suitable for the purpose he had in mind. Considering how famous Moses had become because he had commanded a world of ignorant people, he undertook to build on this foundation, and had some fools follow him, to whom he persuaded that the Holy Spirit was his father and that a virgin was his mother[47]. These good people, accustomed to paying for dreams and reveries, gave in to this fable and believed everything he wanted, all the more easily because a birth above the order of nature was unheard of. Indeed, to be born of a virgin by the operation of the Holy Spirit was, in their eyes, something more than what the Tartars say of their Genghis Khan and the Siamese of their Sommona-Codom, both of whom had virgins as mothers as well as Jesus Christ, but with the difference that they conceived by the virtue of the sun's rays.

---

47. Celsus says, in Origen, that Jesus Christ came from a small hamlet in Judea, and that his mother was a poor village woman who lived only by her work. That having been convinced of having committed adultery with a soldier named Panther, she was chased away by her fiancé, who was a carpenter by profession. That after this affront, wandering miserably from place to place, she secretly gave birth to Jesus. Later, Jesus, finding himself in need, was forced to go to Egypt, where, having learned some of the secrets that the Egyptians make so much of, he returned to his own country, where, proud of the miracles he was able to perform, he proclaimed himself to be God.

This prodigy happened at a time when the Jews, tired of their God, as they had been of their judges[48], wanted to have a visible God, as did the other nations.

As the number of fools is infinite, he found subjects everywhere; but his extreme poverty was an invincible obstacle to his elevation. The Pharisees, sometimes delighted by the boldness of a man of their own sect[49], sometimes jealous of his audacity, would either deprive him or elevate him according to the fickle mood of the populace. Thus, no matter what rumors were circulating about his divinity, it was impossible, being devoid of everything as he was, for his plan to succeed. When he would have made the miracles which one allots to him, having neither money nor army, he could not fail to perish. But with money and troops, it is probable that he would have succeeded no less well than Moses, Mohammed and those who had the ambition to rise above the others. If he was more unfortunate, he was no less skilful, and some places in his history show that the greatest fault of his policy was that he did not provide enough for his safety. Besides, I do not see that he took his measures more badly than those two other legislators, whose memory has remained the arbiter of the beliefs of so many peoples.

---

48. In the 4th Book of Samuel (4 S, 7), the Israelites, being dissatisfied with the sons of Samuel who judged them, asked for a king, following the example of the other nations, to whom they wanted to conform.

49. Jesus Christ was of the sect of the Pharisees, that is to say of the wretched. Whereas the Sadducees were the sect of the rich.

CHAPTER VIII
ON THE POLITICS OF JESUS CHRIST

I. Is there anything, for example, more subtle than what he says about a woman caught in adultery? The Jews, having asked him whether this wretch should be stoned to death, instead of answering yes or no, and thus falling into the trap that his enemies were setting for him, the negative being directly against the Law, the affirmative convincing him of rigor and cruelty, which would have alienated him. Instead, I say, of distributing as a common soul would have done, he says: let him who is without sin cast the first stone[50]. A skilful answer which showed his presence of mind.

II. Another time, it was asked to him if it was allowed to pay the tribute to Caesar[51], or not. Another question which one made to him to surprise him. Because, if he answered no, he was guilty of lèse-majesté, and if he answered yes, he gave damage to the freedom of his nation. He answered neither yes nor no, but said to those who questioned him: «Show me the coin that is given for the tribute. Then, questioning them in his turn, he asked them of whom the image and the inscription, which he saw on this coin, were? Caesar,» they answered. Render

---

50. Jn 8; Mt 22, 17-22.
51. Mt 22:17-22.

to Caesar, he replied, what belongs to Caesar, and to God what belongs to God. By this Norman answer, if it is permitted to speak thus, he evaded the difficulty that was being made to him and avoided the trap in which any other than him would have fallen.

III. He also cleverly avoided another trap that the Pharisees set for him. They asked him by what authority he was instructing and catechizing the people. At first, entering into their thinking, which tended only to convince him of falsehood, either he answered that it was by human authority, because he was not of the sacred body of priests of the old Law, nor of those who were charged with the instruction of the people, or he boasted that he was preaching by express order of God, his doctrine being opposed to the Law of Moses.

To get out of this predicament, he decided to embarrass them by asking them in whose name they thought John was baptizing. The Pharisees, who were opposed to John's baptism as a matter of policy, would have condemned themselves by admitting that he was baptizing in the name of God. On the other hand, if they did not confess it, they would have exposed themselves to the rage of the people, who imagined the opposite. To get out of this predicament, they answered that they did not know anything about it, to which Jesus Christ replied that he was not obliged to tell them either by what authority or in whose name he was preaching.

IV. Such were the tricks and defeats of the destroyer of the old Law, and the father of the new. Such were the seeds of the new religion which was built upon the ruins of the old, where, to say it with a disinterested mind, there is nothing more divine than in the other sects which preceded it. Its founder, who was not altogether ignorant, seeing the extreme corruption of the republic of the Jews, judged it to be near its end and believed that another should rise from its ashes. The fear of being prevented by more ambitious people than himself, made him hasten to establish himself by means quite opposite to those of Moses. Moses began by making himself terrible and formidable to the other nations. Jesus Christ, on the contrary, drew them to him by the hope of the advantages of another life, which they would obtain, he said, by believing in him; whereas Moses promised only temporal goods to the observers of his Law, Jesus Christ made them hope for goods which would never end. The laws of the one looked only at the exterior, those of the other go as far as the interior. They praise or blame even the thoughts and take in everything the opposite of those of Moses. From this it follows, as Jesus Christ believed with Aristotle, that religion and States are like other individuals, which are generated and corrupted; and as nothing is made except from what is corrupted, so no Law succeeds another which is not completely opposed to it. But since it is very difficult to persuade men to change from one Law to another, and since most minds are extremely stubborn in matters of religion, Jesus Christ, in imitation of other innovators, had recourse to miracles, which have always been the pitfall of the ignorant and the refuge of the ambitious.

V. By this means, Christianity was founded, and Jesus Christ, taking advantage of the errors of Moses' policy, succeeded in no place so happily as in the measures he took to make his Law eternal. The Hebrew prophets thought they were doing Moses honor by predicting a successor who would resemble him, that is, a Messiah great in virtue, powerful in goods, and terrible to his enemies. However, their prophecies produced the opposite effect; many ambitious people took the opportunity to call themselves the promised Messiah, which caused revolts that lasted until the complete destruction of this ancient republic.

Jesus Christ, more skilful than the Mosaic prophets in cutting off the feet of those who would rise up against him, predicted that such a man would be the great enemy of God, the delight of demons, the drain of all vices and the desolation of the world[52]. After these fine words of praise, there is, in my opinion, no one who would want to call himself Antichrist; and I do not see that a better secret can be found than this

52. Mt 24, 4.3.24-26; 2 Thes 2, 3-10; 1 Jn, 2, 18.

one, to eternalize a Law; although there is nothing more fabulous than the rumor that is spread about this so-called Antichrist.

St. Paul said that he was already born during his lifetime, and therefore that the advent of Jesus Christ was just around the corner[53]. However, it is more than sixteen hundred years since the prediction of the birth of this forerunner, without anyone having heard about it.

I admit that some have borrowed[54] these words from Ebion and Cerinthus, two great enemies of Jesus Christ, because they fought against his alleged divinity. But it can also be said that if this interpretation is in conformity with the meaning of the apostle, which is not believable, these words designate an infinite number of Antichrists in all the centuries, and there is no true scholar who believes that he or she is harming the truth by saying with Boniface VII[55] and Leo X[56] that the history of Jesus Christ is a fable and that the Law is nothing but a tissue of reveries that ignorance has put into vogue and that interest maintains.

VI. It is nevertheless claimed that a religion which subsists on such flimsy foundations, and whose preachers have been men who are ignorant to the point of stupidity, is a religion which is entirely divine and supernatural; as if one were unaware that there are no people better suited to give vent to the most absurd opinions than women and idiots. It is no wonder, then, that Jesus Christ did not choose scholars and philosophers as his apostles. He knew that his Law and common sense were diametrically opposed, that is why he declaims in so many places against the wise and excludes them from his kingdom, where he

---

53. Th. 2, 7.

54. The original text reads "appropriate".

55. Boniface VIII said, that men have the same souls as beasts, and that these human and beastly souls do not live more than each other. That the Gospel, as well as all other laws, teaches many truths and many lies. For example, a Trinity, which is false, the birth of a virgin, which is impossible, the incarnation and transubstantiation, which are ridiculous. I do not believe in the Virgin any more than in a donkey, nor in her son than in the foal of a donkey.

56. Leo X, entering one day a cabinet where treasures were displayed, exclaimed: "This fable of Jesus Christ helps us to be rich.

admits only the poor in spirit, the simple and the foolish[57]. Therefore, reasonable minds do not think themselves unhappy to have nothing to do with fools.

VII. It would be going too far beyond the limits we have set ourselves in this writing if we were to report here all the other features of his policy. Those who want to know more need only read the New Testament. It is there that one will see how carefully he avoided performing his miracles in the presence of unbelievers and the enlightened, and how skilfully he modelled his Law on that of Moses. At first he protested that far from having the intention of abolishing the latter, he had come expressly to fulfill it. But as the number of his followers increased, he dispensed with its observance, dispensed his disciples from it, and praised them when they had violated it. Imitating in this the new princes, who promise to confirm the privileges of their subjects, while their power is not yet well established, but who violate their promises as soon as they feel strong enough to do so with impunity. Or rather, doing like those clever monarchs who, under the pretext of confirming and explaining the old ordinances of their predecessors, abolish them entirely, and imperceptibly substitute their new laws in their place.

----

57. The Christian belief and doctrine are strange and fierce to the reason and judgment of man. They are contrary to all philosophy and discourse of reason, as can be seen in all the articles of faith, which cannot be understood nor comprehended by human understanding, indeed they seem to him impossible and strange. St. Paul says that if a man wants to consult and hear philosophy and measure things with the compass of reason, he will leave everything and laugh at it as if it were madness. This is the admission made by Charron in a book entitled *Les Trois Vérités* (p. 180 of the Bourdeaux edition, 1593).

CHAPTER IX
ON THE MORALS OF JESUS CHRIST

I. As for the morality of Jesus Christ, if we distinguish that which was particular to him from that which was common to him with the philosophers, we will find that that which is particular to him has two considerable defects. The first is that it demands of men things that are absolutely impossible and against their nature, such as the obligation to hate oneself, to love one's enemies, and not to resist the wicked. The second is that it seems to have been devised with a view to maintaining a group of beggars and country bumpkins, such as his apostles and disciples were. Indeed, is it not filled with perpetual imprecations against the harshness of the rich? Do we not find in it lessons in living at the expense of others? Forms of blessings for cities, towns, villages, houses, people who would welcome the troop, and curses against places that would not receive it.

II. With regard to the other part of his morality, what can we see that is more divine than in the writings of the ancients? Or rather, what do we see that is not an extract, or at least, an imitation?

Saint Augustine[58] admits that he found the whole beginning of the Gospel of Saint John in some of their writings. Joint, that it is found,

---

58. Book VII, chap. IX. and XX. of his *Confessions*.

that this apostle was so much in possession of plundering the authors, that he did not make difficulty to steal from the prophets their enigmas and their visions, to make his apocalypse.

Where does the conformity between the doctrine of the Old Testament and that of Plato come from, if not from the fact that the rabbis, and those who have formed the Scriptures from a collection of fragments, have plundered this great philosopher?

Certainly, the birth of the world is more plausible in his *Timaeus* than in Genesis. However, it cannot be said that this is because Plato read the Judaic books on his trip to Egypt, as Ptolemy, says St Augustine[59], had not yet had them translated when Plato went there. The description that Socrates gives to Sinimias, in the *Phoedon, is* infinitely more graceful than the terrestrial paradise; and the Androgyne is without comparison better invented than all that Genesis says about Eve's extraction from one of Adam's ribs. Is there anything more similar than these two conflagrations, that of Sodom and Gomorrah, and that caused by Phaeton? Joseph and Hypolyte? Nebuchadnezzar and Licaon? Tantalus and the evil rich man? The manna of the Israelites and the ambrosia of the gods? Saint Augustine[60], Saint Cyril and Theophilact compare Jonah to Hercules, nicknamed Trinoctium, because he was three days and three nights in the belly of a whale. The River of Daniel, represented in chapter VII of his Prophecies, is a visible imitation of the Periphlegeton, which is spoken of in the Dialogue on the Immortality of the Soul.

The original sin and Pandora's box are very similar, the sacrifice of Isaac and Jephthah is similar to that of Iphigenia, in whose place a hind was substituted. What is said about Lot and his wife is completely consistent with what is said about Baucis and Philemon. Finally, it is constant that we find between the authors of Scripture, Hesiod and Homer a very great relationship.

---

59. Book VII, chap. IX. and XX. of his *Confessions.*
60. Book VI, chap. XIV. of the *City of God.*

III. But let us return to Jesus Christ. Celsus showed, according to Origen[61], that he had drawn his most beautiful sentences from Plato: a camel would rather pass through the eye of a needle than it is easy for a rich man to enter the kingdom of God[62].

It is to the sect of the Pharisees, of which he was a member, that those who believe in him owe their belief in the immortality of the soul, the resurrection, hell, and most of his morals, in which nothing is more admirable than in those of Epictetus, Epicurus and many others. The latter was proposed by St. Jerome as a man whose virtue put the best Christians to shame, observing that all his works were filled with nothing but herbs, fruits, and abstinence, and whose voluptuousness was so tempered that his best meals were only a little cheese, bread and water. With such a frugal life, this philosopher, all pagan that he was, said that it was better to be unfortunate and reasonable than rich and opulent without having the right reason; adding that it is rare that fortune and wisdom are found in the same subject, and that one could not be happy nor live with pleasure as long as our felicity is accompanied by prudence, justice and honesty, which are the qualities of the true and solid voluptuousness

As for Epictetus, I do not believe that any man, I do not exclude Jesus Christ, was more austere, more firm, more equal, and more free from passions than he was. I am not saying anything that is not easy to prove. But for fear of overstepping the limits I have set for myself, I will only give one example of his constancy from the beautiful actions of his life. When he was the slave of a freedman named Epaphroditus, who was captain of Nero's guards, the brute took it into his head to twist his leg. Epictetus, noticing that he was enjoying it, said with a smile that he could see that the game would not end until he had broken his leg. Indeed, the thing having arrived, as he had predicted it; hey well! continued he, of an equal and laughing face, had I not well said that you would break my leg? Was there ever such constancy as this? And can we say that Jesus Christ went that far? He who wept and

---

61. Book VI, *Against Celsus.*
62. Lk 18:4.

sweated with fear at the slightest alarm given to him, and who showed a lowliness of soul in his death that was not seen in most of his martyrs.

If the insult of time had not robbed us of the book that Arrien had made of the life and death of our philosopher, I am sure that we would have many other examples of his patience. I have no doubt that it will be said of this action what the ignorant say of the virtues of philosophers, that it is a virtue of which vanity is the mother, and which is not indeed what it seems. But I am not unaware either that those who say this are saving it for the pulpit, knowing that :

This is where right or wrong, they have the right to say anything.

I also know that when these cathedrals, these salesmen of air, wind, and smoke, have declaimed with all their might against the avengers of right reason and of outraged virtue, they believe they have earned the money that the States give them to instruct the people. It is so true that nothing in the world comes close to the morals of true scholars than the actions of those ignorant people who decry them and who seem to have studied only to reach a position that gives them bread. A position which they idolize and which they applaud when they have obtained it. Believing then that they have reached a state of perfection, although for those who obtain it it is only a state of self-love, of ease, of pride, of voluptuousness, where most of them follow nothing less than the maxims of the religion they preach. But let us leave these people, who do not know what virtue is, to examine the dogma of the divinity of their master.

Chapter X
On the Divinity of Jesus Christ

I. The most ignorant of the Hebrews, having given the most vogue to the Law of Moses, were also the first to run after Jesus Christ. And as the number of them is infinite, and they love one another, it is not surprising that its errors have spread so easily. It is not that there is not much to suffer with the innovators, especially when they are poor and powerless; but the glory that one hopes for softens the difficulties. Thus, the disciples of Jesus Christ, as miserable as they were following him, often reduced to feeding on grains of wheat[63] that they dropped from the ears, and to seeing themselves shamefully excluded from the places[64], where they thought they were entering to rest from their labors, did not begin to be repulsed until they saw their master in the hands of the executioners and unable to give them the goods, the splendor, the greatness, which he had promised them.

After his death, his disciples, in despair at seeing their hopes frustrated and pursued by the Jews who wanted to treat them as they had treated their master, made a virtue of necessity and spread through the lands, where, on the report of a woman[65], they spread his resurrection,

---

63. Lk 6:1.
64. *Ibid.* 9, 52-53.
65. Jn 20:18.

then his divine filiation and all those fables, which determined the emperor Julian to abandon the sect of the Nazarenes, that is to say Christianity, which he regarded as a crude fiction of the human mind, because he found it founded only on a simple narration of prodigies.

The difficulty they had in advancing among the Jews made them resolve to seek out the Gentiles, and to try whether they would be happier among them than among those of their nation. But, as this required more knowledge than they had, the Gentiles having among them philosophers, too fond of the truth to give themselves up to trifles, they won over a young man of a bold[66] and active spirit, a little better educated than fishermen or rather, a greater babbler. This young man, having associated himself with them by a stroke of heaven which made him blind, because without that the deceit would not have succeeded, attracted to Jesus Christ some simple souls by the account of this vision and by that of his alleged rapture in heaven, by the fear of the punishments of a hell drawn from the fables of the ancient poets, by the hope of a glorious resurrection and a paradise, which is hardly more bearable, than that of Mahomet. So that both of them gave their master the honor of passing for a God, which he himself during his lifetime had not been able to obtain. In what his fate was not better than that of Homer, six of the cities[67] which had chased and despised this poet during his life having disputed after his death the glory of having been his cradle.

II. We can see from this that Christianity depends, like everything else, on the whims of men, in whose opinion everything is considered good or bad according to the mood they are in.

But, moreover, if Jesus Christ were God, it would follow, as Saint John says[68], that God would have been made flesh and would have taken on human nature, which contains as great a contradiction as if one were to say that the circle took on the nature of the square, or that

---

66. The original spells "bufflant".
67. After his death, seven cities claimed the honor of his birth.
68. Jn 1, 1-14.

the whole became part. Indeed, what could be more absurd than to imagine, as Christians do, that the most high God, as they speak, the only infinitely perfect being, came down from the highest of his glory to come and live with beings who differ infinitely more from him than the vilest insects differ from the greatest monarchs of the universe?

That he has taken the weak, the despicable, the miserable nature of these beings, only to redeem them from the slavery and tyranny of one of his rebellious subjects, whom he himself holds in chains, as if he had no other means of taking them away from this enemy of the human race, who can do nothing without him, than that of degrading himself in such a strange way, and even then to save only one of these wretches, against a million he lets perish ? That he has lowered himself to this point only to avenge the insults he had received from these ants, these worms, and to take satisfaction from them as if he could be offended by them? That finally, in order to obtain from his irritated divinity the forgiveness of their alleged offenses and to satisfy his infinite justice, which demanded their death, he himself gave himself up in their place to the most cruel and infamous torture, as if, supposing that he had been really offended, he would not have been master, either to release his rights, or to reconcile these sinners with his divinity in another way, or finally to grant them a free pardon?

But I am ashamed to dwell any longer on such palpable contra-dictions. I will now move on to Mohammed, who deserves to be mentioned, since he founded a Law on maxims which are completely opposed to those of the Christian legislator.

Chapter XI
About Mohammed

I. No sooner had the disciples of Jesus Christ extinguished the Mosaic Law, in order to introduce the Christian one, than men, according to their ordinary caprice, submitted to the Laws of a new legislator who rose by arms as Moses had done. The specious title of prophet and envoy of God[69] did not escape him either. He was no less skilled

---

69. A friend of the famous Golius, having asked him what the Mohammedans said about their prophet, this learned professor in Arabic sent him the following extract, which contains a summary of the life of this impostor, taken from a manuscript in Turkish. The Lord Muhammad Mustafa, of glorious memory the greatest of the prophets, was born in the fortieth year of the empire of Anuschirwan the just. His Holy Nativity came on the twelfth day and the second series of the month of Rabia. Now, after the fortieth year of his age had passed, he was divinely inspired, received the crown of prophecy and the robe of legation, which were brought to him from God by the faithful messenger Gabriel, with the command to call men to Islam. After receiving this inspiration from God, he stayed in Mecca for thirteen years. He left Mecca at the age of fifty-three on the eighth day of the month of Rabia, which was a Friday, and took refuge in Medina. Now it was there that ten years after his retirement, on the twentieth day of the eleventh month and in the sixty-third year of his blessed life, he came to the enjoyment of the divine presence. Some say that he was born while his father Abdalla was still alive, others say that he was born after his death. Lady Amina, his mother, daughter of Wahibe, gave him a nurse, Lady Halima of the tribe of Beni-Saad. Abdo' Immutalib his grandfather gave him the blessed name of Muhammad. He had four sons and four daughters. The sons were Kasim, Ibrahim, Thajib and Thahir, and the daughters Fathima, Ommo Keltum, Rakia and Zeineb. The companions of this august messenger of God were Abubeker, Omar, Osman and Ali, all of them of sacred memory.

at performing miracles and thereby appealing to the weakness of the people, who love the marvelous. At first, he saw himself, like them, escorted by an ignorant populace, to whom he spoke the new oracles that he received from heaven. These sensual and coarse people, lured by pleasures of their own taste, which this impostor promised them in a paradise where the happiness of those who observed his Law would consist in part in that which most flatters the senses, spread his fame far and wide, and exalted it to such an extent that that of his predecessors diminished little by little.

II. As soon as he began to rise and his name became famous in Arabia, Coreïs, a powerful Arab, jealous that a man of nothingness had the audacity to abuse the people, declared himself his enemy and crossed his company. But the family of Coreis having had the upper hand, Mohammed saw himself followed by a crowd of peoples, who, believing him to be a divine man, blindly embraced his new Law. Defeated by such a formidable enemy, he feared only his companion. Lest he should discover his impostures, he thought of warning him; and to do so more surely, he amused him with beautiful promises and swore to him that he only wanted to become great in order to share with him a good to which he had contributed so much. We touch, he said to him, at the happy moment of our elevation[70]. We are followed by a great people whom we gained; but it is a question of confirming it by the artifice that you so happily invented. At the same time, he persuaded him to hide in the oracle pit, from the bottom of which he usually counterfeited the voice of God. This poor man, lured by

---

70. Naudé reports this fact somewhat differently. He says that Mohammed persuaded [the] most faithful of his servants to go down to the bottom of a well which was near a main road, in order to shout when he passed in the company of a great multitude of people who usually followed him. Mohammed is the beloved of God, Mohammed is the beloved of God, and this having happened in the way he had proposed, he suddenly thanked the divine goodness for such a remarkable testimony and asked all the people who were following him to fill up this well and to build a small mosque over it, as a mark of such a miracle. And by this invention, this poor servant was knocked out, and buried under a hail of stones which took away from him the means of ever discovering the falseness of this miracle. But the earth and the babbling feathers received the sound.

the sweet words of this deceiver, counterfeited the oracle as usual; and when he heard the voice of Mohammed, and the noise of the multitude that followed him, he began to shout as he had agreed with him: I, who am our God, protest to you that I have established Mohammed to be the prophet of all nations. From him you will learn my true Law, because the Jews and Christians have altered the ones I gave them.

This man had been playing this role for a long time, but at last he was paid for it in a most ungrateful manner. For Mohammed, hearing the voice that proclaimed him a divine man, turned to the people, who were infatuated with his false merit, and commanded them in the name of God, who recognized him as his prophet, to fill in with stones that pit, from which such an authentic testimony had come out in his favor, in memory of the stone that Jacob once raised on a similar occasion as a sign that God had appeared to him.

Such was the fatal end of this wretch who had contributed to the exaltation of Mohammed; and it is on this heap of stones that the last of the most famous impostors established his Law.

This foundation is so solid that after more than a thousand years of reign, it is not perceived as being ready to be shaken.

III. Thus rose Mohammed. Happier than Jesus Christ, he saw in his lifetime the progress of his Law. Happier even than Moses, who through an excess of ambition rushed into his last days, he died in peace, filled with glory and assured that his doctrine would survive after his death, because he had adapted it to the genius of his followers, born and bred in ignorance and sensuality.

This, readers, is the most remarkable thing that can be said about these four famous legislators. They are as we have portrayed them to you. It is up to you to see if they deserve that you imitate them, and if you are excusable for letting yourselves be led by guides that ambition has raised up and that ignorance perpetuates.

To give more weight to what we have said about religions, legislators, politicians, superstitious people and the foolish credulity of the people, it would be easy for us to show, by an infinite number of testimonies, that our sentiments on this subject are perfectly in conformity with those of the best authors, both ancient and modern, who have written on these matters. But as these testimonies would take up too much space, we will limit ourselves to reporting what two famous modern[71] have written on these articles. Although both are ecclesiastics, and consequently obliged to keep a distance from superstition, one will nevertheless not fail to notice, through their gentleness and their Catholic style, that they say things as freely and as strongly as we do. You will judge for yourselves, by reading the following, which we have faithfully extracted from their works[72].

---

71. Pierre Charron and Gabriel Naudé.
72. The following chapters, from the ELEVENTH to the SEVENTEENTH, are taken word for word from the Three Truths, by Charron, from *La Sagesse*, and from *Considérations politiques sur les coups d'état* by Naudé.

Chapter XII
Religions

I. There are five religions which have had great credit and reputation in the world, as capitals and masters, introduced one after the other, according to the following order, and what is very remarkable, they were conceived almost in the same place of the earth:

The Natural, beginning with the human race in Palestine;

The Gentile, invented after the Flood and shortly after the reckless company, which built the Tower of Babel, was by the confusion of tongues, and thus younger than Nature and the world, nearly two thousand years before Christ, and put into practice in Chaldea;

The Judaica, conceived in the time of Abraham and with him, about a hundred years after the Gentile, in Palestine, that is, in the same place as the Natural;

The Christian, conceived by Jesus Christ, about four thousand years after the birth of the world in the land of Palestine;

And the Mohammedan in Arabia, six hundred years after the Christian.

These five capital religions, the most famous in the world, have each one under itself several and various kinds of religions: the Gentile mainly; how it had a very great extent, vogue and duration in the world, because not only the means of serving and honoring the deity were different, but it was also divided into several sects with different opinions and beliefs. There are three main forms, which St. Paul seems to have meant when he compared it with Judaism. There is no longer any Greek, Jew, Barbarian or Scythian. That of the Barbarians, without Law, without rule, or certain and prescribed ceremony, adores and serves some feigned deity, each one at his whim. The two others have their sacrifices and services prescribed and certain, but in various ways. The Scythian has them cruel and bloody. The Greek (so called by a particular name, but the most famous, any other sect except the Barbarian and the Scythian) has them more political and humane; and this one again variously, according to the nations and their authors. The Greeks in particular, instructed by their poets and philosophers, the Egyptians by their priests, the Gauls by their druids, the Romans by their Books of the Sibyls, and the Laws of Numa, the Persians by their magicians, the Hindus by their Brahmans and gymnosophists.

The Christianity passes by far all the others in that. And there would be too much to count and make an inventory of all the members and particular differences that are in Christianity. Firstly for the look of the different nations in some points of doctrine, and mainly to the cult and service of God: Greek, Latin, Ethiopian, Syrian, Armenian, Hindu, Muscovite and others.

Then concerning opinions on doctrine and belief, so many heresies and so many sects. Finally, looking at the ceremonies and external means, there is a very great variety of orders, professions, and ways of life. And all these great diversities have been, and still are, under the common flag of their leader, and under the Christian name.

II. These religions debate among themselves and want to defend and authorize themselves for the same reasons. Each one alleges its miracles, its saints, its victories; these are the common weapons. In particular, each one wants to prevail against the others of some right and prerogative. The Natural one of its origin, antiquity and simplicity; which being sufficient, says that all the rest is only addition and over-load, matter of disputes and debates. The Gentile, more polite, braves the sciences, the beautiful speeches and moral and political regulations, by which and with very good grace, is represented the image of virtue; every republic is well trained and well behaved. The Judaica and then the Mohammedan allege for them in common the simplicity of a God, as well in belief as in external representation, against The Christian Trinity and The Gentile Plurality. But the Judaica, moreover, boasts of the antiquity and nobility of its people and race, of the miracles and celestial favors, as much in its establishment and foundation as in its progress, and of the great succession of its prophets. The Mahometan, the last to arrive, is proud of its prosperity and its great victories, having greatly reduced the greatness of the others in a short time, even of the Christian, who alone held the upper hand at the time of its birth; so much so that it is feared by almost everyone.

III. On the other hand, each suffers some reproach from the others: the Natural, that it is not really religion, being vague, uncertain, and having nothing to prescribe or order; the Gentile because of the sacrifices of human bodies, the worship of dumb things, the infamous multitude, genealogy, and accointance of its gods, and the vile and ungrateful obliviousness of the true sovereign God; the Judaic because of its cruelty to its prophets, and that it is a superstitious religion, odious and displeasing to all nations; The Christian because it gives a son equal and companion to God, worships images and the life of Christians is all infected with gambling, chance, adultery and blasphemy; the Mohammedan because of the gross and carnal vanity that is in it, the Koran being full of unbearable nonsense, and because of its progress and procedure, which is all by the sword, wars, murders, captivity.

However, the professors hate, despise and scorn each other, holding each other blind, cursed, doomed and lost; even chasing each other like angry and rabid dogs.

Chapter XIII
On the Diversity of Religions

I. First of all, it is a terrible thing that the great diversity of religions, which has been and is in the world, and even more so that the strangeness of some of them, so fantastic and exorbitant. How wonderful it is that human understanding could have been so intoxicated with impostures. For it seems that there is nothing in the world, high or low, which has not been deified in some place and which has not found a place to be worshipped.

II. They all agree in many things, have almost the same principles and foundations, agree on the thesis, hold the same progress and walk on the same foot. All of them find and provide miracles, prodigies, oracles, mysteries, sacred, prophets, festivals, certain articles of faith and belief necessary for salvation. All have their origin and beginning small, weak, humble, but little by little, by a contagious continuation and acclamation of the peoples, with fictions put forward, have taken root and have been authorized, so much so that all are considered with affirmation and devotion, even the most absurd. All of them hold and teach that God is appeased, bowed and won by prayers, presents, vows and promises, feasts, incense. All believe that the main and most pleasant service to God, and the powerful means of appeasing him, and of practicing his good grace, is to take pains, to carve out, to impose, and to burden oneself with difficult and painful work. For witness, everywhere in the world, in all religions, so many orders, companies, and brotherhoods destined to certain and various exercises, very painful and of extravagant profession, tear and cut up their bodies, and think by this to deserve much more than the common people, who do not soak in these afflictions and torments like them. Every day new ones arise, and human nature will never cease and see an end to inventing ways to give itself pain and torment. This comes from the opinion that God takes pleasure and delight in the torment and defeat of his creatures, which opinion is fundamental to the sacrifices, which were universal throughout the world, before the birth of Christianity and exercised not only on innocent beasts which were slaughtered with the shedding of their blood as a precious gift to the divinity, but (a strange thing of the intoxication of the human race) on children, small, innocent, and made men, both criminals and good people, a custom, practiced with great religion by all nations; gestures, which among other ceremonies and sacrifices, send to their god Zamolxix, from five to five years, a man of them to ask him for the necessary things. And so that he dies in the moment, they expose him to death in a doubtful way, which is to throw him on the points of three straight javelins. They dispatch several of them in a row, until one locks himself in a deadly place, and suddenly expires, considering that one to be clean and favored, the others not. Persians, witness Amestris, mother of Xerxes, who at once buried alive fourteen youths of the best houses, according to the religion of the country. Ancient Gauls, Carthaginians who immolated their children to Saturn in front of their fathers and mothers; Lacedemonians who mignified their Diana by having young boys whipped in her favor, often to death. Greeks, witness the Sacrifice of Iphigenia, Romans, witness the two Decies. *Quae fuit tanta iniquitas Deorum, ut placari à Pop. Rom. non possent, nisi tales viri occidissent.* Mohammedans who scar their faces, stomachs, and limbs, to gratify their prophet. The New Indies, East and West, and in Themistitan cement their idols with the blood of children.

What alienation of sense, to think of flattering the divinity with inhumanity, paying divine goodness with our affliction and satisfying his justice with cruelty? Justice therefore hungry for human blood, innocent blood drawn and shed with so much pain and torment, *ut sic Dii placentur, quemadmodum ne homines quidem saeviunt*[73]. Where does this opinion and belief come from, that God takes pleasure in the torment and defeat of his works and of human nature? According to this opinion, of what naturalness must God be?

III. The religions also have their differences, their particular and separate articles, by which they distinguish themselves from each other, and each one prefers itself to the others, and boasts of being the best and truest of the others, and also reproach each other with something, and thereby condemn and reject each other.

IV. But as they are born one after the other, the youngest always builds on its elder, it neither improves nor condemns its elder from top to bottom, otherwise it would not be heard and could not take root, but only accuses it, or of imperfection, or of its finished term, and that on this occasion she comes to succeed her and perfect her, and thus ruins her little by little and enriches herself with her spoils, as the Judaica did to the Gentile and Egyptian, the Christian to the Judaica, the Mahometan to the Judaica to the Christian together. On the other hand, the old ones condemn completely and entirely the young ones, and hold them as capital enemies.

V. All religions are strange and horrible to the common sense, because they propose and are built and composed of parts, of which some seem to the human judgment, low, unworthy and of which the spirit a little strong and vigorous makes fun of; or too high, brilliant, miraculous and mysterious where the man cannot know anything. Now the human mind is only capable of mediocre things, despises and disdains the small ones, and is astonished and disinterested in the great

---

73. Senec.

ones; for which it is marvelous if it does not reject, disgust, and lose interest in any religion where there is nothing mediocre and common. For if he is strong, he scorns it and laughs at it; if he is weak and superstitious, he is surprised and scandalized by it. *Praedicamus Jesum Crucifixum, Judaeis scandalum, gentibus stultitiam.* Hence it is that there are so many unbelievers and irreligious people, because they consult and listen too much to their own judgment, wanting to examine and judge matters of religion according to their own scope and capacity, and to deal with it by their own natural tools. It is necessary to be simple, obedient, and debonair in order to be fit to receive religion, to believe and keep oneself under the Laws, by reverence and obedience, to subject one's judgment and to allow oneself to be led and conducted by public authority, captivantes *intellectum in obsequium fidei.*

VI. But it was necessary to proceed in this way, otherwise the religion would not be in respect and admiration, as it should. Now it is necessary that with difficulty, authentically and reverently, it is received and sworn. If it were of human and natural taste without strangeness, it would be much more easily, but less reverently taken.

VII. Now being religions and beliefs, strange to the common sense, far surpassing all human reach and intelligence, they must not and cannot be taken, nor lodged with us by natural and human means (otherwise so many great, rare and excellent souls as there have been would have arrived there) but they must be brought and leased by extraordinary and celestial revelation, taken and received by divine inspiration, and as if coming from heaven Thus all those who hold it, and believe it, and use this jargon, which comes neither from men, nor from any creature, but from God.

VIII. To tell the truth, without flattering or disguising anything, it is nothing of the kind; they are, whatever one may say, held by human hands and means. For witness the way religions have been received in the world and are still received every day by individuals. The nation, the country, the place give the religion; one is of that which the place where one is born and brought up holds, we are circumcised, baptized, Jews, Mohammedans, Christians, before we know that we are men. The religion is not of our choice and election. To witness the life and the manners so badly in agreement with the religion, the human and very light occasions, which go against the content of its religion. If it were held and planted by a divine attachment, nothing in the world could shake us from it; such an attachment would not break so easily; if there were touch and ray of the divinity, it would appear everywhere and effects would be felt and would be miraculous.

If you had a single drop of faith, you would move mountains. But what proportion and propriety is there between the persuasion of the immortality of the soul and of a future reward so glorious and happy, or so unhappy and distressing, and the life one leads? The mere apprehension of the things which one says one so firmly believes, would cause one to go astray and lose one's sense. The mere apprehension and fear of dying by justice, and in public, or of some other shameful and untoward accident, has made many lose their sense, and has thrown them into very strange parties. Is this the price of religion that teaches the future? Would it be possible to believe in the truth and hope for this blessed immortality, and fear death, a necessary passage to itself? To fear and apprehend this infernal punishment and live as one does? These are tales, things more incompatible than fire and water. They say that they believe it; they make believe that they believe it, and want to make believe it to the others, but it is not, and they do not know what it is to believe. They are mockers and confronters, said an elder.

Chapter XIV
Divisions of the Christians

I. What has always been found strange and distasteful in the Christian religion, and of which people have been most astonished and offended, are the great divisions which are and have always been in it. For not only did the foreigners and unbelievers, her enemies, object to joining her, but also her servants, were scandalized by it, and some used it for their evil purposes. We learn from the Book of the Acts of the Apostles, and from several places of St. Paul, that from the beginning of Christianity and from the time of the Apostles, which is the primitive Church, there were great differences, schisms and divisions, not only of the police, but also of the doctrine. Shortly afterwards, St. Clement Alexandrian, Origen's teacher, wrote that the Jews and Gentiles reproached the Christians for attributing to themselves the truth and the knowledge of salvation. All accused and condemned each other of errors and heresies. For this reason they should not believe, nor seek the truth except from themselves, being so discordant.

Since the emperor Julian the Apostate, finding dissensions between the Christians (says his historian Marcellinus), studied to nourish them in order to weaken them and so that they could not rise and prevail against him. After him, the emperor Valence, a Christian, then made an Arian, used (says the ecclesiastical history) as an excuse for his apostasy, the great differences, schisms, and debates that existed among the Christians. After all these, St. Augustine said that in his time the Church of Jesus Christ had come to such a height of authority that all her enemies and slanderers were confused and rendered mute, and that they had nothing left to say against the Christians, except that they were not in agreement, and that the Gentiles, who remained, had nothing to object to but their dissensions. It is indeed strange that the Christian religion, which being the only true one in the world, the revealed truth of God, should be united in faith, as there is only one God and one truth, should nevertheless be torn into so many parts, and divided into so many opinions, and contrary sects, so that there is no article of faith, nor any point of doctrine, which has not been variously debated and agitated, and there have not been heresies and contrary sects. And what makes it even stranger is that in the other false and bastard religions, Gentile, pagan, Judaic, Mohammedan, such divisions and partiality are not found. And if there are divisions, they are few, slight, and of little importance, as in the Judaic and Mohammedan, or if they have been many, as in the Gentile, among the philosophers, at least they have not produced great and striking effects and stirrings in the world. This is nothing compared to the great and pernicious divisions that have existed in Christianity from the very beginning and ever since.

II. For if we look at the effects produced by the divisions of Christianity, it is a terrible thing. Firstly, as regards the police and the State, there have often been alterations and subversions of republics, kingdoms and races, divisions of empires, up to a universal change of the world, with cruel, furious and more than bloody exploits, to the great scandal, shame and reproach of Christendom. In which, under the title of zeal and affection for religion, each side mortally hates all the others, and it seems to him that it is possible to do all acts of hostility, something which is not seen in other religions. Only Christians are allowed to be murderers, treacherous, and treacherous, and to lash out at each other with all kinds of inhumanity, against the living, the dead, honor, life, memory, and spirits, the sepulchres and ashes, by fire, iron, very stinging libels, curses, banishments from heaven and earth, digging up, sacking[74] of bones and monuments, provided that it is for the safety or advancement of his party, and the reversal of the other ; And this without composition, with such rage, that all consideration of kinship, alliance, friendship, merit, obligation is set back. He who yesterday was praised to the skies, and described as great, learned, virtuous, wise, today putting himself in another party is decried, proclaimed ignorant, wicked, unhappy. There is zeal and ardor of religion, out of there, everywhere else in the observance of religion, coldness. Those who are moderate and restrained are noted and suspected of being lukewarm and unzealous. It is an abominable fault, to make good face and kind treatment to those of the opposite party. Some are scandalized by all this, as if the Christian religion taught us to hate and persecute, and served us as a broker, to put to work and make our passions of ambition, avarice, revenge, hatred, spite, cruelty, rebellion, sedition. Which, moreover, are not so well managed, as being awakened by the fact of religion.

From which, however, some say, that one should not attack religion, but religious people; and those say that according to the rule of charity, and the discourse of reason to the faults of the understanding and judgment, which are called errors, false opinions, that one should not be carried by hatred and rigor, but by pity and compassion ; and to treat these wandering and unbelieving people as one does the lame, deaf, blind, frantic, whom one does not hate, but pities; one pities them and helps them. It is enough to behave with them in this way, that one does not approve of their opinions at all. One should not avoid them or greet them, which is a form of hatred, incivility and enmity, and even less hostility against the person, but a disapproval, an open[75] disagreement of opinions and claims.

It seems to some others that this is not done without some good reason, which is that Christians espouse their religion and embrace it as a truth given by the hand of God, of which they are extremely jealous and careful; from which it happens that to all those who undertake

---

74. The original text reads: "rustling".
75. The original text reads: "disconsent".

anything against it to disturb it, offend, insult it, they resent it and attack it mortally as if they were the sworn and capital enemies of God, their salvation, and all the rest. For they cannot, nor should they behave coldly and moderately, without betraying the cause of God and their own.

And if the same is not true of other religions, it is because they do not hold their religions in the same rank, nor do they make such a statement, they know that religion is a human thing and received from the hands of men. Since it does not concern the police and the State, but rather the soul and conscience, other worse effects come out of it, which are disturbances of the conscience, interest in religion itself, disorders of morals and discipline, so much so that finally, many, weary and bored with so many divisions and contrasts, not knowing what to resolve and what to stand for, leave everything, remain blank and come to despise and abandon religion. For we know only too well that apostasy, atheism and irreligion are the products and the little bunkers of heresies. Moreover we know that the divisions, which have been in Christianity in the East, have served as an opportunity, and have opened the door to Mohammed and his Koran.

Chapter XV
Superstitious people, superstition and credulity of the people

I. The superstitious person does not let either God or men live in peace; he fears God, grieving, displeased, difficult to please, bland to anger, long to appease, examining our actions in the human way of a very severe judge, spying on us and watching us at the step; which he testifies enough by his ways of serving him. He trembles with fear, cannot trust or be sure, fearing that he has never done well enough, and that he has omitted something, for which omission everything may be worthless; He doubts whether God is pleased, takes pains to flatter him to appease him, to win him over, pesters him with prayers, vows, offerings, feigns miracles to himself, easily believes and receives the supposed ones from others, takes for himself and interprets all purely natural things as expressly made and sent by God, bites and runs at everything that is said, like a very anxious man, *duo Superstitiosis propria, nimius timor, nimius cultus*

What is all this, if not by taking great pains, vilely, sordidly, and unworthily to act with God and more mechanically than one would with a man of honor? Generally all superstition and fault in religion comes from not esteeming God enough, we call him back and swallow him up, we judge him according to our own moods. What blasphemy!

II. Now this vice and disease is almost natural to us and we all have some inclination to it. Plutarch deplores the human infirmity which never knows how to keep measure, and to remain firm on its feet.

III. It is also popular, comes from the weakness of soul, of ignorance or ignorance of God very gross; of which it is found more willingly in the children, women (*pro devoto fœmineo sexu*), old people, sick, assailed and beaten of some violent accident. In short to the Barbarians. *Inclinant natura ad superstitionem Barbari*[76].

IV. In addition to these natural seeds and inclinations to superstition, many hold it in their hands and favor it for the gain and great profit they derive from it. The great and powerful, though they know what it is, do not wish to disturb or prevent it, knowing that it is a very proper tool for leading a people; whence it happens that they not only foment and warm up that which is already in nature, but also when there is need, they forge and invent new ones, like Scipio, Sertorius, and others *who faciunt animos humiles formidine Divum, depressosque premunt ad terram. Nulla res multitudinem efficacius regit, quam Superstitio*[77].

V. The people (by this word I mean the gathered vulgar, the peat and popular dregs, people, under whatever cover of low, servile and mechanical condition) is a many-headed beast, vagrant, wandering, mad, dizzy, without conduct, without spirit, nor judgment.

If Postel persuades him that Jesus Christ only saved men and that Mother Jeanne must save women, he will suddenly believe him. That David George claims to be the son of God, he will adore him. Let an enthusiastic and fanatical tailor counterfeit the king in Munster and say that God has destined him to punish all the powers of the earth, he will obey him and respect him as the greatest monarch in the world. Let father Domptius tell him that the Antichrist is coming, that he

---

76. Plutarch in *Sertorio*.
77. Curtius.

is ten years old [and] has horns, he will testify to be afraid of him. If impostors and charlatans call themselves brothers of the Rosicrucians, he will run after them. If he is told that Paris will soon be destroyed, he will run away. That the whole world must be submerged, he will build arches and boats early so as not to be surprised. That the sea must dry up and that wagons can go from Genoa to Jerusalem, he will prepare himself to make the trip.

Let them tell him the fables of Melusine, of the wizards' sabbath, of the werewolves, of the goblins, of the fairies, of the gods, he will admire them. That the womb torments some poor girl, he will say that she was possessed, or will believe in some ignorant or wicked priest, who makes her pass for one. If some alchemist, magician, astrologer, lullist, cabalist, starts to cajole him a little, he will take them for the most learned and honest people in the world. Let a Peter the Hermit come to preach the crusade, he will make relics of the hair of his mule. If someone laughingly tells him that a duck or a bird is inspired by the Holy Spirit, he will seriously believe it. If a plague or a storm ruins a province, he will suddenly blame it on greasers or magicians. In short, if he is deceived today, he will still allow himself to be surprised tomorrow, never taking advantage of past encounters to govern himself in the present or future; and in these things consist the principal signs of his great weakness and imbecility.

VI. As for his inconstancy, we have a beautiful example in the Acts of the Apostles, in that the inhabitants of Lystria and Derben had not seen St. Paul and St. Barnabas before, *that levaverunt vocem suam Lycaonicè dicentes: Dii similes facti hominibus descenderunt ad nos; et vocabant Barnabam Jovem, Paulum quoque Mercurium*[78] ; and nevertheless incontinent afterwards here *that lapidant Paulum, traxerunt eum extra Civitatem, existimantes mortuum esse*[79]. The Romans adore Sejan in the morning, and in the evening:

---

78. They raised their voices and said in the Lycaonian language: the gods have come down to us in the form of men; and they called Barnabas Jupiter, and Paul, Mercury.
79. They stoned Paul and dragged him out of the city, thinking he was dead.

Ducitur unco Spectandus.
(Juven. Sat. 10)[80].

The Parisians do the same with the Marquis d'Ancre; after having torn the dress of the father of Jesus Maria, to keep the pieces as relics, they make fun of it two days later. If he gets angry, it will be like the young man of Horace,

Iram
colligit et ponit temere, et mutatur
in horas (ad Pison)[81].

If he meets some man of authority when he is in his most ebullient mutiny and sedition, he will flee and abandon everything; if some reckless or bold beggar comes along who puts his heart in his stomach and his fire in his spleen, he will return more furious than before; in short, we can particularly attribute what Seneca said (*De Vita B.* Chap. XXVIII) of all men, *fluctuat, aliud ex alio comprehendit, petita relinquit, relicta repetit, alternae inter cupiditatem suam, et paenitentiam vices sunt*[82].

---

80. He is dragged with a hook to serve as a spectacle to the people.
81. Easily angered and calmed, and changes at any time.
82. He is always in doubt, he always makes new plans, he leaves what he had asked for, and he immediately asks again for what he has just left: desire and repentance command in him in turn, and possess one after the other the domination of his soul.

Chapter XVI
On the origin of monarchies

I. If we consider the beginnings of all monarchies, we will always find that they began with some inventions and deceptions, making religion and miracles walk at the head of a long succession of barbarities and cruelties. It is Tite-Live (1.4., decadence I.) who first made the remark: *Datur haec venia antiquitati, ut miscendo humana divinis, primordia Urbium augustiora faciat*[83].

What we will show hereafter will be true, but for the time being, we must remain in the general and begin our proof with the establishment of the four first and greatest monarchies of the world.

The fame of the queen Semiramis, who founded the empire of the Assyrians, was industrious enough to persuade her people that having been exposed in her infancy, the birds had taken care to feed her, bringing her the beakful as they are wont to do to their young, and wanting to confirm this fable by the last actions of her life, she ordered that one makes the rumour after her death that she had been converted into a pigeon and that she had flown away, with a great quantity of birds which had come to seek her even in her room.

---

83. It is allowed to antiquity that by mixing human things among the divine ones, it makes by there more august the beginnings of the cities.

She had again the resolution to feign and change sex, and of woman that she was to become male, playing the character of her son Ninus and forging him in all his actions. And to better come to an end of this enterprise, she decided to introduce a new kind of clothing among the people, which was largely favorable to cover and hide what could most easily make recognize a woman. *Brachiaenim ac crura velamentis, caput tiara tegit, et ne novo ha-bitu aliquid occultare videretur, eodem ornatu populum vestiri jubet, quem morem vestis exinde gens universa tenet*[84], et par ce moyen *primis initiis Sexum mentita, puer credita est. (Just. initio.)*[85].

Cyrus, who established the monarchy of the Persians, also wanted to authorize himself by the vine that his grandfather Astyages had been born ex naturalibus filiae, cujus palmite omnis Asia obumbrabatur[86]*, and of the dream that he himself had when he took up arms, and that he chose a slave as a companion for all his undertakings; but he was even more convincing in his opinion that a bitch had fed him and nursed him in the woods, where he had been exposed by Harpagon, until a shepherd, having met him by chance, brought him to his wife, and had him carefully fed in her house.*

For Alexander and Romulus, as their designs were higher, also judged that it was necessary to practice more and much more powerful stratagems. That is why they began as well as the preceding ones with the fable of their origin; they carried it however as high as it could be done, from where Sidonius had the occasion to say:

Magnus Alexander, nec
Romanus habentur
Concepti serpente Deo[87].

---

84. For she covered her arms and legs with a robe, and her head with a turban; so that she would not seem to hide anything under this new garment, she ordered that all her people take similar ones, which fashion this people still keeps.
85. In the beginning, having disguised herself, she was taken for a boy.
86. Of his daughter, whose shadow of oaths covered all Asia.
87. The Great Alexander and the Roman are believed to have been conceived from a serpent and a god.

For Alexander, he made believe that Jupiter was accustomed to come to see and to rejoice with his mother Olympias under the figure of a snake. And when he came into the world, the goddess Diana so assiduously attended the birth of the aforementioned Olympias, that she did not think of helping the temple which she had in Ephesus, which in the meantime was entirely consumed by a fortuitous blaze.

What more? In order to better establish the opinion of his divinity in the belief of his subjects, he arranged the priests of Jupiter Ammon in Egypt, *ut ingredientem Templum statim ut Amnonis Filium salutarent* (Justin 1.11.)[88] ; and to better play his character, *Rogat num omnes Patris sui intersectores sit ultus; respondent Patrem ejus nec posseinterfici, nec morii*[89]. He even came to the effects, ordering Parmenion to demolish all the temples, and to abolish the honors which the people of the East returned to Jason, *ne cujusquam nomen in Oriente venerabilius quam Alexandri esset*[90].

Let us add to that that certain captives having given him the knowledge of the remedy which one could be used against the poisoned arrows of the Indians, he made believe before that God had revealed it to him in dream. But this insatiable greed having led him to make himself adored, he finally recognized by the admonitions of Callisthenes, by the obstinacy of the Lacedemonians and by the wounds which he received every day while fighting, that all his forces would never be sufficient to be able to establish this new apotheosis, and that it is necessary a greater fortune to gain a small place in the sky, than to dominate here below and dominate all the earth.

If one wants to add to these stories those of the death of his father Philip, to which he consented with his mother Olympias, and that also of Clytus, whom he killed with his own hand, because he had acquired too much authority between the soldiers, one will find that Alexander

---

88. That as soon as he entered the temple, they would greet him as the son of Jupiter Ammon.

89. He asked if he had not taken revenge on all the murderers of his father, and they answered that his father could neither be killed nor die.

90. So that there was no name in the East more venerable than that of Alexander.

practised in secrecy what Caesar did since quite openly: *Si violandum est jus, regnandi causa*[91].

As for Romulus, he put himself in credit by the stories of the god Mars, who practiced familiarly with the mother Rhea; by that of the she-wolf who nourished him; by the deception of the vultures, the death of his brother, the asylum which he established in Rome, the kidnapping of the Sabines, the murder of Tatius which he let go unpunished and finally by his death by drowning himself in marshes, to make believe that his body had been taken in the skies, since it could not be found on earth. Now if one adds to these coups of Romulus, those that Numa-Pompilius his successor practiced by means of his nymph Egeria and the superstitions that he established during his reign, it will be easy then to judge:

Quibus auspiciis illa inclita Roma
Imperium Terris animos aequavit Olympo?[92]. *(Virgil)*

If we wanted to examine all the other monarchies and all the states which are inferior to these four, we could fill a large volume with similar histories. Therefore, it will be enough for the last proof of our maxim, to examine what Mohammed practiced at the establishment not less of his religion, than of the empire, which is today the most powerful in the world. Certainly, as all the great spirits (Postellus and Alii) have always had the industry of taking advantage of the most signal disgraces which happened to them, this one wanted to do the same; so that seeing that he was very prone to fall badly from above, he took it into his head to make his friends believe that the most violent paroxysms of his epilepsy, were so many ecstasies and signs of the spirit of God which descended in him; He also persuaded them that a white pigeon which came to eat grains of wheat in his ear was the angel Gabriel who came to announce to him on behalf of the same God what

---

91. If you have to break the law, you have to rule.
92. By what means this famous Rome has mastered the whole earth, and has carried its ambition as high as Olympus.

he had to do; then, he used the monk Sergius to compose a Koran, which he pretended to be dictated to him from the mouth of God; Finally, he attracted a famous astrologer to dispose the people by the predictions he made of the change of state that was to come and of the new Law that a great prophet was to establish, in order to receive his own more easily when he came to publish it. But having once noticed that his secretary Abdalla Bensalon, against whom he had been wrongly piqued, was beginning to discover and publish such impostures, he slit his throat one evening in his house and had him set fire to the four corners, with the intention of persuading the people the next day that this had happened by fire from heaven, and to punish the said secretary who had endeavored to change and corrupt some passages of the Koran

It was not, however, to this finesse that all the others were to lead, but one more was needed to complete the mystery, and that he persuaded the most faithful of his servants to descend to the bottom of a well which was close to a main road, in order to cry out when he passed by in the company of a great multitude of people who usually followed him, «Mohammed is the beloved of God, Mohammed is the beloved of God». And this having happened in the way he had proposed, he suddenly thanked the divine goodness for such a remarkable testimony, and prayed all the people who followed him to fill up this well at the same time and to build above it a small mosque as a mark of such a miracle. And by this invention this poor servant was buried under a hail of stones which took away from him the means of ever discovering the falseness of this miracle.

Excepit sed Terra sonum,
calamitous loquaces[93].

---

93. But the earth and the babbling feathers received the sound. Petronius in *Epigrams*.

Chapter XVII
Legislators, politicians and how they use religion

I. All the ancient legislators who wanted to authorize, establish, and properly found the laws that they gave to their peoples, had no better way of doing so, than by publishing and making people believe with all possible industry that they had received them from some deity, Zoroaster from Oromasis, Trismegistus from Mercury, Zamolxis from Vesta, Charondas from Saturn, Minos from Jupiter, Lycurgus from Apollo, Drago and Solon from Minerva, Numa from the nymph Egeria, Mahomet from the angel Gabriel ; and Moses, who was the wisest of them all, describes in Exodus how he received his immediately from God.

In consideration of the fact that the reign of the Jews is entirely ruined and abolished, *mansit tamen,* says Campanella, *religio mosaica cum superstitione in Hebraeis et Mahumetanis, et cum reformatione praeclarissima in Christianis*[94]. It is, as I believe, what gave Cardan cause to advise princes, who for being little advantaged by birth or deprived of money, supporters, military forces, and soldiers, cannot govern their

---

94. However the Mosaic religion remained with superstition among the Jews and the Mohammedans, and with a very beautiful reformation among the Christians. In *Aphorism. polit.*

States with enough splendor and authority, to lean on religion, as David, Numa, and Vespasian did in the past and very fortunately.

II. But as there have never been more than two means capable of keeping men in their duty, namely, the rigor of the tortures established by the ancient legislators to repress the crimes, of which the judges could be aware; and the fear of the gods and their thunderbolts, to prevent those of which, for lack of witnesses, they could not be sufficiently informed, in accordance with what the poet Palingenius says (in *Libra*):

Semiserum vulgus fraenandum est relligione
Pœnarumque metu, nam fallax atque malignum.
Illius ingenium est semper, nec sponte movetur
Ad rectum[95].

The same legislators have also recognized that there was nothing that dominated the minds of the people more violently than this one, which, when it comes to being the object of some action, suddenly brings all the pursuit that can be made of it to a head; Prudence turns into passion, anger, if there is any, turns into rage, all conduct goes to confusion, the very goods and life are not put into consideration, if it is necessary to lose them to defend the divinity of some monkey's teeth, of an ox, of a cat, of an onion, or of some other idol even more ridiculous, *nulla siquidem res efficacius multitudinem movet quam Superstitio*[96].

III. Legislators and politicians have used religion in five main ways, under which all the others can be understood:

The first, the most common and ordinary, was to persuade their people, that they had the communication of the gods, to come more

---

95. It is by religion and by the fear of torments that it is necessary to restrain the half savage rabble, because its spirit is always deceitful and malignant, and of itself does not lead to what is right.

96. There is nothing that makes the rabble act more effectively than superstition. Q. Curt. Free IV.

easily to the end of what they had the will to execute. As we see that in addition to the ancients that we have reported above, Scipio wanted to make believe that he did not undertake anything without the council of Jupiter Capitolinus, Sylla, that all his actions were favored by Apollo of Delphi, of which he always carried a small image; and Sertorius, that his hind brought him the news of all that was concluded in the Council of the gods.

But to come to the stories which are closer to us, it is certain that by similar means James Bussularius dominated for some time in Pavia, John of Vicenza in Bologna, and Jerome Savonarola in Florence, from whom we have this remark of Machiavelli: «The people of Florence are not stupid[97] «, to whom nevertheless brother Jerome Savonarola made well believe that he spoke to God. Not more than sixty years ago, Guillaume Postel wanted to do the same in France, and recently Campanelle in Upper Calabria; but they could not succeed, any more than the previous ones, because they did not have the strength in hand; because, as Machiavelli says, this condition is necessary for all those who want to establish some new religion.

IV. The second invention which politicians have used to take advantage of religion among the people, has been to feign miracles, find dreams, invent visions, and produce monsters and prodigies:

Quae vitae rationem vertere possent ;
Fortunasque omnes magno turbare timore[98].

Thus we see that Alexander, having been informed by some physicians of a sovereign remedy against the poisoned arrows of his enemies, made them believe that Jupiter had revealed it to him in a dream. And Vespasian attracted people who pretended to be blind and lame, so that he could cure them by touching them. It is also for this reason that Clovis accompanied his conversion of so many miracles; that

---

97. On Tite-Live.
98. That can change the way of life and disturb all fortunes by a great fear.

Charles VII increased the credit of Jeanne la Pucelle, and the emperor of at present that of the father of Jesus Maria, hoping perhaps to gain still some battle not less than that of Prague.

V. The third is based on false rumors, revelations, and prophecies that are deliberately spread to frighten, astonish, and shake the people, or to confirm, embolden, and encourage them, depending on the opportunities to do one or the other. And on this subject, Postel remarks that Mohammed maintained a famous astrologer, who did nothing else but preach a great revolution and a great change which were to be made, as much in religion as in the Empire, with a long succession of all kinds of prosperities, in order to clear by this invention the way for the same Mohammed and to prepare the peoples to receive more willingly the religion that he wanted to introduce, and by the same means to intimidate those who would not want to approve it, by the suspicion that they could have to fight against the order of the destinies by opposing this new favorite of the sky, this one being always the most advantaged:

Cui militat aether
et conjurati veniunt ad Classica venti[99].

It was by means of these crazy beliefs that Ferdinand Cortez occupied the Kingdom of Mexico, where he was received as if he had been the Topilchin, whom all the soothsayers had predicted would soon arrive. And Francis Pizarro in the Kingdom of Peru, where he entered with the general applause of all the peoples, who took him for the one whom the Viracocha had to send to deliver their king from captivity. Charlemagne himself penetrated Spain by means of an old idol, which, as the soothsayers had foreseen, dropped a large key that it held in its hand; and the Arabs or Saracens coming, under the leadership of Count Julian, to flood the same Kingdom of Spain. There was hardly

---

99. For whom heaven fights, and the winds with one accord come to the sound of his trumpets.

any thought of repelling them, because some time before they had seen their faces depicted on a canvas that was found in an old castle near the city of Toledo, where it was believed that she had been locked up by some great prophet. And I dare say with many historians that without these beautiful predictions, Mohammed II would not have so easily taken the city of Constantinople. But do we want a more remarkable example than the one that happened in the year 1613, concerning Ascosta, the main city of the Isle Magna, which having rebelled against the Sophi, was taken without much difficulty by his lieutenant Arcomat, and this in virtue of a certain prophecy received by tradition among the citizens, which said, that if this city did not surrender to Arcomat, it would be arcomaté, that is to say, if it did not surrender to Dissipe, it would be dissipated. If it had wanted to defend itself, it might not have been taken, since according to the report of Garcias ab Horto, a Portuguese doctor who had been written there thirty or forty years earlier, the city contained five places of tower, fifty thousand fires, and gave to the Sophi 15 million six hundred thousand ecus each year of assured income.

It is therefore a great way open to politicians to deceive and seduce the silly populace to use these predictions to make them fear or hope, receive or refuse, whatever they want.

VI. But the fourth means, which is that of having preachers and making use of well-disciplined men, is still much shorter and more certain, for there is nothing that cannot easily be overcome by this stratagem. The force of eloquence and of a fancy and industrious speech, flows with such pleasure in the ears that it is necessary to be deaf or finer than Ulysses not to be charmed by it; also it is true, that all that the poets wrote of the twelve labors of Hercules finds its mythology in the various effects of eloquence, by the means by which this great man came to the end of all kinds of difficulties; This is why the ancient Gauls were right to represent him with many small gold chains which came out of his mouth, and went to attach to the ears of a great multitude of people whom he dragged in chains after himself.

To speak only of France, do we not know that this famous crusade undertaken with so much zeal by Godfrey of Bouillon was persuaded and concluded by the harangues and preaching of a simple man called Peter the Hermit, as the second was by those of Saint Bernard.

What more could there be? Was there ever a more wicked and abominable murder than that of Louis, Duke of Orleans, committed in 1407 by the Duke of Burgundy? Nevertheless, he found Master Jean Petit, theologian and great preacher, who knew how to palliate, cover and disguise it so well by the sermons he gave in Paris on the square of Notre-Dame, that all those who wanted to support the party of the house of Orleans were held by the people to be mutineers and rebels; which forced them to use the same artifice as their enemy, and to put themselves under the protection of that great man of good, Jean Gerson, who undertook their defense, and made the Council of Constance declare the proposal held by Petit as heretical and erroneous. But as John Petit had been the cause of great evil under Charles VI, there was a brother Richard, a cordelier under Charles VII, who was also the cause of great good; for in ten preachings of six hours each that he made in Paris, he had all that there were of tables, aprons, cards, marbles, billiards, dice, and other games, of fate or of chance, which lead and violate men to swear and blaspheme, thrown into fires lit on purpose at the crossroads; but this good man was not so soon out of Paris that they began to despise and mock him openly, and the people returned with more application than before to their ordinary entertainments.

Neither more nor less than the strange metamorphoses, and the miraculous conversions, if one must say so, that the Capuchin father Giacinto da Casale did not twenty years ago through all the cities of Italy where he preached, lasted only as long as the aforementioned father remained there to exercise the functions of this office.

VII. The fifth invention, which has always been the most common, and the most subtly practiced, is to undertake under the pretext of religion what no other could make valid and legitimate. Indeed, the proverb commonly used by the Jews, *in nomine Domini committitur omne malum*[100], is no less true than the reproach which Pope Leo made to the emperor Theodosius, *privatae causae pietatis aguntur obtentu, et cupiditatum quisque suarum religionum h-bet velut pedisequam*[101].

Since the examples are so common, that all the books are full of them, I will be satisfied, after having spoken enough about our French, to stop here on the Spaniards, and to follow punctually what Mariana, the most faithful of their historians, has noticed.

He thus says, speaking of the first Goths who occupied Spain, and of the wars which they made to drive out one another, that they used religion as a pretext to reign, and his ordinary refrain is *optimum fore judicavit religionis pretextum*[102], speaking of king Sisenand who was assisted by the Arian Burgundians to drive out king Suinthile; and when it is question of the kings of Chintila, *cum species religionis obtenderetur*[103] ; as well as describing in what way Ervige had driven out king Wambe, *Optimum visum est religionis speciem obtendere*[104] ; and when two brothers of the house of Aragon, *violento imperiosi Pontificis mandato*[105], armed themselves against each other, this good father remarks very appropriately that there was nothing more inhuman than to violate the laws of nature in this way, *sed tanti fides religioque fuere*[106] ; and the same still speaking about Navarre, which Ferdinand *immensa imperandi ambitione*[107], took away from his own niece, he adds for excuse, *sed species religionis praetexta facto est, et Pontificis jussa*[108]. But because it would never be done to want to allege all the places where this brave author Mariana made similar remarks, I will attest that his

---

100. Under the name of God all kinds of evil are committed.
101. Private matters are dealt with under the pretext of religion, which each one makes serve his lusts.
102. He judged that the pretext of religion would be very good. Book VI, chapter V.
103. When religion was paraded. Chap. V.
104. It was found very good to make parade of the religion. Chap. VII.
105. By a violent order that an imperious pope gave (it was Boniface VIII).
106. But faith and religion had so much strength. Book LI, chap. I.
107. By the immense ambition that he had to command all.
108. But he covered himself with the pretext of religion and the orders of the pope. Book XXV, last chapter.

whole book is full of them. Passing to Charles V, I will produce against him what Francis I said in his apology of the year 1573, Charles wants to encroach on the States under the color of religion.

Speaking of the war in Germany, the emperor, under the color of religion and armed with the League of Catholics, wants to oppress the other and make the way for the monarchy. This was also very well noticed by Monsieur de Nevers.

Finally when the late King James was called to the Crown of England, the King of Spain hastened to form a close alliance with him; The Constable of Castile was sent there, the relation of it was printed, and Rovide, senator of Milan, calls this alliance a very holy work, recognizes the king of England for a very holy Christian prince, offers him on behalf of the king his master all his forces by sea and by land, and protests that the king of Spain does it *divina admonitione, divina voluntate, divina ope, non nisi magno Dei beneficio*[109].

As it is the nature of most princes to deal with religion as charlatans, and to use it as a drug, to maintain the credit and reputation of their theater, one should not, it seems to me, blame a politician, if in order to come to grips with some important matter, he resorts to the same industry, although it is more honest to say the contrary, and to talk about it in a healthy way,

Non sunt haec dicenda palam,
prodendaque vulgo,
Quippe hominum plerique mali,
plerique scelesti[110].

This is enough, in my opinion, to make our case to those who would accuse us of having gone too far. Let us now resume the thread of our discourse, which we will be grateful to have interrupted in this way.

---

109. By divine warning, by divine will, by divine assistance, and as by a great grace of God.

110. One should not discover or reveal such things to the common people, seeing that among men there are so many wicked and scoundrels. Palingenius, in *Libra*.

Indeed, besides the fact that the extracts we have given from Charron and Naudé are excellent in themselves, they are perfectly suited to the aim we have set ourselves in this writing, to combat superstition.

To cure yourself of this disease, read the following with a free mind, but read it carefully, and you will infallibly experience that it is the pure truth.

Chapter XVIII
Sensible and obvious truths

I. Moses, Numa-Pompilius, Jesus Christ and Mohammed being as we have presented them to you, it is certain that it is neither in the Laws nor in their writings that you must seek the true idea of God. The divine apparitions and conferences of the first, second and last, and the divine filiation of the third, are impostures which you must flee from if you love the truth.

II. God is a simple being, or an infinite extension, which resembles what it contains, that is to say, which is material, without nevertheless being either just, or merciful, or jealous, or anything that one imagines, and which consequently is neither punisher nor remitter.

This idea of punishment and reward can only fall into the minds of the ignorant, who only conceive this simple being, whom we call God, under images which do not suit him at all. But those who use their understanding, without confusing its operations with those of the imagination, and who have the strength to get rid of the prejudices of a bad education, are the only ones who have a healthy, clear and distinct idea of Him. They consider it as the source of all the beings it produces without distinction, one being no more than the other in its regard, and a man costing it no more to produce than a worm or a flower.

III. Therefore it is not to be believed that this simple and extensive being, which is what is commonly called God, sets more store by a man than by an ant, by a lion than by a stone, and by any other being than by a fetus. Let there be nothing beautiful or ugly about him, good or bad, perfect or imperfect. Let him want to be praised, prayed for, sought after, caressed. That he be moved by what men do or say, susceptible to love and hate, in a word, that he think more of man than of the rest of creatures, whatever their nature. All these distinctions are pure inventions of a narrow mind. Ignorance has invented them and interest foments them.

IV. Thus every man who will make good use of reason will not believe in heaven or hell, nor in souls, nor in gods or devils, in the way they are commonly spoken of. All these big words have been coined only to blind or to intimidate the people. You will be convinced of this if you will take the trouble to go back with us to the source of the error that gave rise to the false ideas that have been attached to these words, and if you substitute the real ones.

V. The infinite number of stars that we see above us have led to the admission of as many solid bodies, where they move, among which there was one destined for the celestial court, where God is like a king in the midst of his courtiers. This is where the abode of the blessed has been established, and where it is pretended that good souls are elevated on leaving the body and this world. But without stopping at such a frivolous opinion, and which no man of good sense admits, it is certain that what is called *heaven* is nothing other than the continuation of our subtler and more refined air, where these stars move without being supported by any solid mass, in the same way that the earth, which is actually suspended in the middle of the air, is moved and agitated.

VI. As one has imagined a heaven, which is, as they say, the abode of God and the blessed, as it was among the pagans, of the gods and goddesses, one has since imagined, like them, a hell or a subterranean place, where the souls of the wicked are said to descend after their death, in order to be tormented there. But this word «hell», taken in its proper and natural meaning, does not mean anything other than a low place, which the poets invented to oppose the dwelling place of the heavenly inhabitants, which they believed to be[111] very high and very high. This is what the word *Inferus,* or *Inferi* of the Latins and that of the Greeks, means, a dark place, such as the sepulchre, and any other low and dark place.

---

111. The original text reads: "feigned".

Chapter XIX
On the soul

I. The soul is something more delicate and more difficult to deal with than heaven and hell. That is why it is appropriate, in order to satisfy the reader's curiosity, that we speak of it a little longer. For this purpose, before saying what it is, we shall report what the most ancient philosophers thought about it, and we shall do so in a few words, so that it will be easier to remember.

Some have said that the soul is a spirit or an immaterial substance, others a particle of the divinity. Some a very subtle air, some a hot wind, some a fire, some a compound of water and fire. Some a fortuitous assembly of atoms, and some a compound of subtle parts, which evaporate and are exhaled, when the man dies. Some have made it consist of the harmony of all the parts of the body, and others in the subtlest part of the blood, which separates in the brain and distributes itself in the nerves. So that the source of the soul, according to the latter, is the heart, where it is generated, and the brain is the place where it performs its noblest functions, because there it is more purified from the gross parts of the blood. Finally, there have been those who have denied that there are souls.

Here are the principal feelings that the ancient philosophers had of the soul. To make them more sensitive, we will divide them into corporeal and incorporeal.

II. Pythagoras and Plato said that the soul is incorporeal, that is to say, a being capable of subsisting without the aid of the body, and which can move by itself. That all the particular souls of animals are portions of the universal soul of the world. That these portions are incorporeal, immortal, and of the same nature as this universal soul of the world, of which they are parcels, similar to a hundred small fires, which are of the same nature as a large one from which they have been taken.

III. These philosophers believed that the universe is animated by an invisible immaterial substance, which knows everything, which is always moving and which, in their systems, is the source of all the movement in the world, and of all the souls, which, according to them, are particles of this substance. Now, as these souls are very pure and infinitely above bodies, they do not unite with them, they say, immediately; but by means of a subtle body, then another a little coarser, and always so by degree until they can unite with the sensible bodies of animals into which they descend as into dungeons or sepulchres. The death of the soul, they add, is the life of the body, where it is as if buried and where it only weakly exercises its most noble functions. On the contrary, the death of the body is, according to them, the life of the soul, because it comes out of its prison, gets rid of matter and reunites with the soul of the world from which it came. Thus, according to this thought, all the souls of animals are of the same nature, and the diversity of their functions comes only from the difference of the bodies where they enter.

Aristotle, in addition to the soul of the world, admits a universal understanding common to all men and which does, with respect to particular understandings, what light does with respect to the eyes, so that in the same way that light makes objects visible, the universal understanding makes objects intelligible. This philosopher, who established the four elements as the principles of all things, could not relate the operations of the soul to any of the elements, and believed that there was a fifth principle, from which it owes its origin. He did not give a name to this fifth principle; but he gives a new one to the soul, which means a perpetual movement or a power that moves eternally, and he defines it as what makes us live, feel, conceive and move. But as he does not say what is this being which is the source and the principle of these noble functions, it is not in him that one must seek the clarification of the doubts which one has on the nature of the soul.

IV. Dicearchus, Asclepius, and in some way Galen, also believed the soul to be incorporeal, but in a different way. Indeed, they said that it is nothing other than the harmony of all the parts of the body, that is to say, what results from the exact mixture of the elements and the disposition of the parts, humors, and spirits. Thus, they say, just as health is not a part of the person who is well, although it is in him, so, although the soul is in the animal, it is not for that reason one of its parts, but a mutual agreement of all those of which it is composed. Whereupon it is to be noticed that these authors believe the soul to be incorporeal, on a principle opposite to their intention. For to say that it is not a body, but only something inseparably attached to the body, is to say, in good school, that it is completely corporeal, since we call corporeal, not only that which is body, but all that is form and accident which cannot be separated from matter.

These are the names of those who believed the soul to be incorporeal or immaterial, who, as you see, are not in agreement with themselves and therefore do not deserve to be believed. Let us come to those who have taught that it is a body.

V. Diogenes believed that the soul is made of air, from which it is inferred the necessity of breathing, and defines it as air that passes from the mouth through the lungs into the heart, where it heats up and from where it is then distributed to all the bodies.

Zeno, founder of the Stoics, believed that the soul or spirit was fire. Leucippus and Democritus also said after him that it is of fire; but they added that like fire, it is composed of atoms, which easily penetrate the parts of the body and make it move.

Hippocrates said that it was a compound of water and fire, Empedocles of the four elements.

Epicurus believed, like Democritus, that the soul is composed of fire, but he adds that in this composition there enters air with steam and another substance, which has no name and which is the principle of feeling. That from these four different substances, a very subtle spirit is formed, which spreads throughout the body, and which must be called the soul.

Aristoxenus, philosopher and musician, said that the soul is a chord of all the parts of the body, or a harmony similar to that which results from the diversity of the voices and the instruments which accompany them.

All these philosophers having noticed that the soul grew and withered with the body; that it was weak in childhood, vigorous in the strength of age, rambling in old age, dreamy in sleep, stupefied in drunkenness, dejected in sickness and moreover that it was corporeal, believed with those who lived before Phecydes that it was mortal[112].

VI. Xenocrates, according to Cicero[113], denied that there were souls, and Dicearchus makes an old man named Pherates say that the soul is nothing and that it is only a name in the air which means nothing. That there is neither soul nor spirit, neither in man nor in beast. That this power by which we act and feel is equal in all that lives, that it is inseparable from the body, and that it is nothing other than the body itself, modified in such a way that it subsists by the temperament that nature has given it.

---

112. Phecydes, a native of the island of Sciros who lived under the reign of Servius Tullius, sixth king of Rome, is, according to Cicero (I. Book of the Tusculanes) the first of the philosophers who maintained that the souls were immortal. He was followed by Pythagoras, his disciple, who came to Italy during the reign of Tarquin the Superb. More than a hundred years later, Plato, having seen in his trip to Italy the Pythagorean philosophers, and among others, Philolaus, Eurythus, Archytas and Timaeus, not only entered into the thought of Pythagoras on the immortality of the soul, but also devised new reasons to support this feeling.
113. Book L of the Tusculanes.

VII. M. Descartes maintains, but pitifully, that the soul is not material. I say pitifully, because never did a philosopher reason so badly on this subject as this great man. Here is how he goes about establishing the immateriality of the soul.

First, he says, we must doubt the existence of all bodies, and believe that there are none, then reason in this way: there are no bodies, yet I am, therefore I am not a body, and therefore I can only be a substance that thinks.

First of all, the doubt he poses is quite impossible, for although we may sometimes not think that there are bodies, it is nevertheless impossible to doubt that there are bodies when we think about them.

Secondly, whoever believes that there is no body, must be sure that there is not one, since no one can doubt himself. But if he is sure, his doubt is useless.

Thirdly, when he says that the soul is a substance, or a thing that thinks, he tells us nothing new; for this is what everyone agrees on. The difficulty consists in determining what this thinking substance is; and he does not explain it.

VIII. In order not to be biased, as he has done, and to give the healthiest idea of the soul that one can have, we shall first of all point out that it is of the same nature both in animals and in man, and that the diversity of its functions comes only from the difference of the organs and humors.

This being said, here is, according to us, what the soul is.

Chapter XX
What is the soul

I. It is certain that there is in the world a very subtle spirit, or a very loose and ever-moving matter, whose source is in the sun and the rest is spread in all the other bodies, more or less, according to their nature, or their consistency.

This is what the soul of the world is, this is what governs it, this is what gives it life, and of which some portion is distributed to all the parts that make it up.

II. This soul is the purest fire in the universe, it does not burn by itself; but it burns and makes its heat felt by the different movements it gives to the particles of other bodies, where it is insinuated.

Visible fire has more of this spirit than air, the latter more than water, and earth has much less. Among the mixtures, plants have more than minerals, and animals even more.

Finally, this fire, being enclosed in the bodies, makes them capable of feeling; and this is what is called soul, or what is called animal spirits, which spread to all parts of the body.

III. it is therefore certain that this soul, being of the same nature in all animals, is dissipated in the death of man, as well as in that of the beasts. Hence it follows that what the poets and theologians sing about the other world is only a chimera that they have forged and told for reasons that it is easy to guess.

Chapter XXI
Of the spirits, which are called demons

I. Although we have spoken at some length about the manner in which the belief in spirits was introduced among men, and have shown that these spirits were only phantoms which existed only in the imagination, yet as men have made this belief a fundamental point of their religion, we have judged it advisable to treat this subject more thoroughly than we have done above. However, as men have made this belief a fundamental point of their religion, we have judged it advisable to treat this subject more thoroughly than we have done above.

For this purpose we shall examine what the philosophers and poets of paganism believed about spirits, and we shall show that it is from them that the Jews have taken what they believe, and that the Christians have taken from them the opinion they have of them. Finally, we shall prove to Christians, by their own principles, that there is no devil.

II. The ancient philosophers were not enlightened enough to explain to the common people what these phantoms were; however, they did not hesitate to tell them what they thought of them. Some of them, seeing that they dissipated and had no consistency, called them immaterial, incorporeal, forms without matter, colors and figures, without being nevertheless bodies, neither colored, nor figured, adding that they could put on air like a suit of clothes, when they wanted to make themselves visible to the eyes of men. The others said that they were animated bodies, but that they were made of air or of another more subtle matter, which they thickened at will when they wanted to appear.

III. If these two kinds of philosophers were opposed in the opinion they had of ghosts, they agreed in the names they gave them; all calling them *demons*. In this they erred as grossly as those who believe that they see the souls of the dead in their sleep, or that it is their own souls that they see when they look in a mirror, or who believe that the stars they see in the water are the souls of those stars.

IV. After this foolish imagination, they fell into an error which is hardly less bearable, when they believed that these ghosts had unlimited power. This is an absurd belief, but one that is common to ignorant people who imagine that what they do not know is some infinite power.

V. This ridiculous opinion was no sooner divulged than the rulers used it to support their authority. They established a belief concerning spirits, which they called religion, in order, as we have already insinuated, after a famous historian of antiquity[114], in order, I say, that the fear that the people would have of these invisible powers would keep them in line. And to do it with more weight, they distinguished the demons in good and bad, those to incite the men to observe their Laws, and these to retain them and prevent them from infringing them.

But, to know what demons are, we must read the Greek poets, and especially what Hesiod says in his *Theogony*, where he deals extensively with the generation and origin of the gods.

---

114. It is Polybius. It is necessary, he says, to admit that if one could form a republic, which was composed only of wise men, all the fabulous opinions of the gods and the underworld would be completely superfluous. But since there is no state whose people are not as we see them, prone to all sorts of disorders and wicked deeds, it is necessary to use to repress them the imaginary fears that religion imprints, and the panic terrors of the other world, which the ancients have so prudently introduced for that purpose.

VI. The Greeks were the first ones who invented them, and from their home they were, thanks to their colonies and their victories, in Asia, in Egypt and in Italy.

It was the Jews, who were scattered in Alexandria and elsewhere, who had knowledge of it. They used it happily like other peoples, but with the difference that they did not call *demons*, like the Greeks, good and bad spirits alike, but only the bad ones, reserving for the good demon the name of *spirit of God,* and calling *prophets* those who had this good spirit. Moreover, they called *divine spirit* what they considered a great good, and *cacodemon*, «evil spirit», on the contrary, everything they considered a great evil.

VII. This distinction of good and evil spirits made them call *demonic* those whom we call lunatics, insane, furious, epileptics, as well as those who spoke an unknown language. A badly made and unclean man was, in their opinion, possessed of a foul spirit, a mute, of a mute spirit. Finally these words of spirits and demons became so familiar to them that they spoke of them in any meeting. Hence, it is evident that the Jews believed, like the Greeks, that ghosts were not pure chimeras or visions, but real beings, which existed independently of the imagination.

VIII. Hence the Bible is full of these words *spirits, demons, demoniacs.* But nowhere is it said how or when they were created. And Jesus Christ is no more excusable in this than he was, since, having often spoken of angels and good and evil spirits, he never said whether they were material or immaterial, which makes it clear that he knew only what the Greeks had taught his ancestors. That if he knew more, he is as blameworthy for not having instructed men as he is for denying them all the virtue, faith and piety that he assures them he can give them. But, to return to the spirits, it is certain that these words *demon, Satan, devil,* are not proper names which designate any individual, and that only the ignorant would ever be capable of believing this on the word of both the Greeks, who invented them, and the Jews who adopted them.

Since these were infected with it, they appropriated these names, which mean wicked, deceitful, cunning, adversary, enemy, accuser, slanderer, destroyer, exterminator, sometimes to the invisible powers, sometimes to their own enemies, that is to say, to the Gentiles, whom they said were living in the kingdom of Satan, since only they, in their opinion, were living in that of God

IX. As Jesus Christ was a Jew, and consequently very imbued with those insipid opinions which his nation had drawn from the Greeks, we read everywhere in the Gospels and in the writings of his disciples these words of *devil*, of *Satan*, of *hell*, as if they were something real and effective. However, it is true, as we have shown, that there is nothing more visionary. But when what we have said would not be enough to prove it, only two words are needed to convince the most obstinate.

All Christians agree that God is the first principle and source of all things, that he created them, that he preserves them and that without his help they would fall into nothingness. According to this principle, it is certain that God created the so-called devil and Satan as well as all other creatures. And whether he created him good or evil, which is not the point here, it follows from this principle that if he subsists, however evil he may be, as they say, it can only be through the intervention and permission of God, who is willing. Now, how can one conceive that God maintains a creature who not only curses him incessantly and hates him mortally, but who also endeavors to debauch his friends, in order to have the pleasure of cursing him with an infinite number of mouths? How, I say, can it be understood that God maintains, preserves and allows the devil to exist, in order to do him the worst he can, to dethrone him if he could, and to turn away from his service his chosen ones and his favorites? What is God's purpose in this? Or rather, what is God's purpose in telling us about the devil and hell? If God can do everything and nothing can be done without him, why does the devil hate him, curse him and take away his friends? Either he agrees or he does not; if he agrees, it is certain that the devil, in cursing him, does only what he must, since he can only do what God wants, and consequently it is not the devil, but God himself who curses himself through the mouth of the devil, a very absurd thing in my opinion. If he does not agree, then it is not true that he is all-powerful. And if he is not all-powerful, then instead of one principle of all things, we must admit two, one of good and one of evil, one who wills one thing, the other who wills and does the opposite. Where does this reasoning lead? To make people admit, without reply, that there is neither God, nor devil, nor soul, nor heaven, nor hell as they are portrayed, and that theologians, that is to say those who tell fables for divinely revealed truths, are all, except for a few ignorant people, people of bad faith, who maliciously abuse the credulity of the people to insinuate what they please, as if the common people were only capable of chimeras, or that they should only be fed with these insipid meats, where they see only emptiness, nothingness, madness, and not a grain of salt of truth and wisdom.

For a long time now, people have been infatuated with the absurd maxim that truth is not made for the people and that they are not capable of knowing it; but at all times, there have also been sincere minds that have protested against such an injustice, as we have just done in this little treatise.

Those who love the truth will undoubtedly find great consolation in this; and it is to these alone that we wish to please, without worrying in any way about those to whom prejudice takes the place of infallible oracles.

END

Table of Contents

9 782315 010981